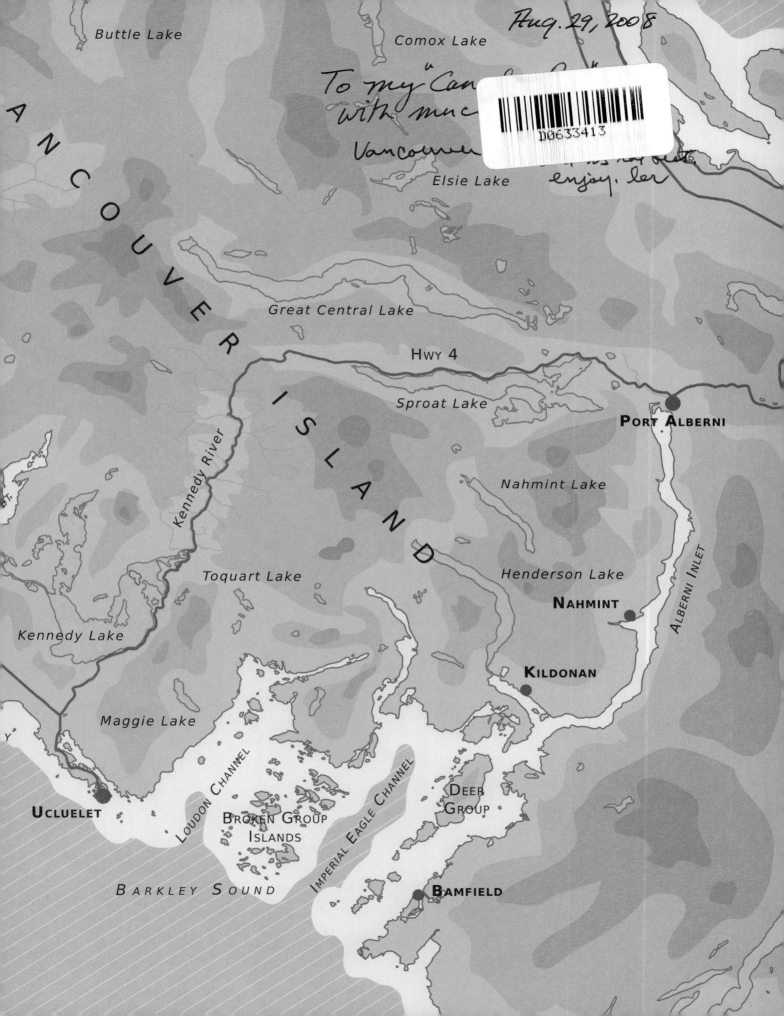

The Wild Edge

The Wild Edge

Clayoquot, Long Beach & Barkley Sound

JACQUELINE WINDH

HARBOUR PUBLISHING

Page 1: Unusual calm on outer
coastal shores by Catface
Mountain, Clayoquot Sound.

Pages 2-3: Lennard Island lighthouse, viewed from Chesterman
Beach at dusk.

Pages 4-5: A full summer moon
rises over the islands of
Clayoquot Sound.

Contents

1
A Savage Beauty

Like the waves that
relentlessly pound
Vancouver Island's outer
shores, the seasons of the
west coast follow a never-
ending circle: a surge of
life and energy that crests
and falls back, year after
year.

Bedwell Lake in Strathcona Provincial Park,
Clayoquot's northern headwaters.

I came here a decade ago, just for the summer. Born inland, I was a stranger to the coast—and it to me. Suddenly I found myself living on an island where the swirling sigh of surf on the rocks outside my door lulled me to sleep each night. Behind my cabin towered trees of unimaginable size. Everything was unfamiliar and new. I did not know the names of the plants, or what berries I could eat. I didn't understand the rhythm of the seasons or the moods of the sea.

To my utter surprise, and against all of my plans, I stayed! As an avid sea kayaker, I found that the mysterious fjords, the sweeping beaches, the tiny islets all begged to be explored, but it was more than that. The Pacific Rim, from the verdant serenity of the rain forest to the formidable power of winter storm waves crashing on rocky outcroppings, replenishes the soul. Clayoquot called to me with its spirit and its vitality. I knew I had found my place.

Now, after 10 years on this coast, I am well into my seemingly endless journey of discovery. I know the patterns of the seasons; I can read the water and the sky. I know where bears can be found from the seasonal foods they follow, and I know what wild foods I can pick and forage for too. I know this small-town community of Tofino and its people. I have friends among the Nuu-chah-nulth, whose ancestors have lived on this land from time immemorial. From them I have learned much: a way of being and a connection to the land that is very hard for people from my culture to comprehend.

A stranger no more, I am part of this place.

More than a million visitors a year cross Vancouver Island, hoping to get to know the Pacific Rim. So many of them ask me, "What should we do while we are here?" All I can say to them is: stay longer.

You cannot hope to know this sprawling and diverse land in a few days. Not even in a week or a year. I have spent a decade here, exploring on foot and by kayak, combing the most remote inlets, paddling the least visited stretches of outer coast, battling to make any progress at all through tangles of devil's club and salmonberry bushes, in a quest to know this place. I have learned to listen, and I have learned to see.

With this book, I am sharing with you the mystery and charm of Vancouver Island's central west coast, from the wild and hidden secrets of the Hesquiat Peninsula south to the wave-pounded islets at the entrance to Barkley Sound, and from the lofty, craggy peaks of the central mountains down the forested slopes to the rugged Pacific shores.

I hope that this book will give you some idea of the complexity and the allure of the wild West Coast—its savage beauty and fascinating history, and the people who make their home here. I want to show you the places that you don't make it to (this time!), as well as to give you greater insight into the places that you do see. And I hope to inspire you to help protect it, so that this ancient and venerable land and its traditional inhabitants will be here for all future generations, and to tread lightly on the many other wild lands in peril on our planet.

Opposite: The falls at Shark Creek, behind Flores Island, plunge straight into the ocean.

A hummingbird perches on a salal bush.

Following pages: Sand-pipers are seasonal visitors to the coast, stopping on beaches and mud flats to feed while travelling to and from Arctic breeding grounds.

the wild edge

Wya Point, at the south end of Florencia Bay, is one of many spectacular vantage points for winter storm-watching.

Vancouver Island grey wolves, a distinct sub-group of the wolf family, are commonly sighted on West Coast beaches.

Spring seems always to arrive on the West Coast as a surprise. The monotony of winter, with the grey skies spitting out grey sheets of rain, suddenly ceases. The sun peeks tentatively through the clouds, still low in the sky. Local residents materialize on the beaches, taking advantage of the lengthening days. Almost overnight, yellow flower spikes of skunk cabbage appear poking up through the mud, and pink buds of salmonberry flowers burst open on naked branches.

On some particular day in March, the tree frogs decide that they must sing, and an incessant chorus begins in the ponds and ditches. As the frogs begin their serenade, the first gray whales pass by offshore, travelling northward from breeding grounds in Mexico. Most will continue to Alaska, but a few regulars stop here, remaining in shallow bays to feed throughout the summer. In Tofino and Ucluelet, tour boat operators clean up their boats and put them back in the water in preparation for the first wave of whale-watchers.

The Nuu-chah-nulth called this time *Ayaqamilth*, or "moon of herring spawn," for the dense schools of small, silvery Pacific herring that flood into the bays and inlets to spawn. Following the traditions of their ancestors, modern Nuu-chah-nulth submerge hemlock boughs weighted down with stones in anticipation of the returning fish. The herring lay their eggs in thick, sticky masses on the fronds. The roe, a delicacy known as *qwakmis*, may be peeled off the branches and popped in the mouth fresh, or it may be dried or frozen for later use. Humans are not the only ones who savour this treat. Gray whales gather in Hesquiat Harbour, and squawking swarms of seagulls descend into Hot Springs Cove, all relying upon this rich food that marks the end of winter.

Top: Salmonberry blossoms, one of the first signs of spring.

Bottom: Eggs of Pacific herring, a Nuu-chah-nulth delicacy, are collected on hemlock branches submerged in the water.

With the arrival of spring, the rain forest comes alive with birdsong. Although many forest birds remain on the coast over winter, they do not announce their presence with song. Thrushes, wrens and towhees flit silently through the undergrowth, searching for seeds and insects under dead leaves on the forest floor. The lengthening days break the serious mood, and suddenly the forest echoes with these birds' melodies. The eerie whistle of the varied thrush wavers in treetops, and winter wrens launch into a boisterous canto that belies the fact that their lungs cannot be any larger than a pea. The arrival of the migrants only adds to the concert, with the trill of yellow warblers high in the trees, and the rapid whirring and peeping of the rufous hummingbirds' aerial mating dance.

Waves of migratory birds also appear overhead. By April, *Hoqamilth* ("flying flocks moon") in the Nuu-chah-nulth calendar, the skies echo with gentle honking as vees of geese incessantly fly northward. Flocks of sandpipers and other shorebirds alight on the beaches and tidal mud flats, many of them having flown non-stop from tropical wintering grounds. They may stay for a week or more, feeding in order to replenish their energy for the second leg of their journey as they continue to summer breeding grounds in the Arctic. By early May the shorebirds number in the tens of thousands. The flocks rise together as if choreographed, twisting and turning in unison to display rippling waves of white bellies and tan backs. Birdwatchers with tripods supporting heavy telescopes and cameras observe respectfully from the shorelines, recording arrival and departure dates and noting rare species.

Pungent skunk cabbage
flowers are among the
first harbingers of spring.

Juvenile Pacific tree frog
sitting on a blade of grass.

Preceding pages: The moods of Chesterman Beach change constantly, according to season and weather.

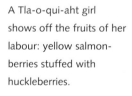

A Tla-o-qui-aht girl shows off the fruits of her labour: yellow salmonberries stuffed with huckleberries.

As the days grow warmer, black bears emerge from wintering dens and descend to the shores of the inlets. They satisfy their burning spring hunger with whatever they can find, grazing on grass and clover, flipping over rocks at the tide line in search of purple shore crabs, and gorging on the first salmonberries that appear in May and June. Scrawny black cubs trot after their mothers, rapidly learning about foraging in the wild as they fatten and grow. Crows bicker with one another as they follow the shoreline patrol, picking up scraps left by the bears.

The green of spring slides into summer shades of blue and gold. By June, the rocky shorelines are a riot of colour, with masses of scarlet Indian paintbrush and yellow monkey flower and cinquefoil. Clusters of white bunchberry flowers sprout from mossy logs. Bald eagles busy themselves ferrying strips of fish to hungry nestlings. By the end of the month, the giant young birds perch clumsily on the edge of the nesting platforms, flapping awkwardly as they get used to the feel of the huge wings with which they will soon soar through the air.

Human visitors flood into the region. The beaches are alive with colour as people enjoy their favourite activities—surfing, swimming, cycling along the packed sand,

picnicking and simply strolling to admire the seashells and inhale the salt sea breeze. By night, beach fires crackle and the smell of cedar smoke wafts through the air. Sea kayakers take advantage of calm ocean conditions and relatively stable weather, bobbing up and down on outer coastal waters or slipping silently up sheltered inlets. The outer seaboard buzzes with the unending din of motors as whale-watching vessels, water taxis and sport fishing boats ply the coastal waters and float planes drone overhead.

In the outer waters, the humpback whales have arrived, working together in tight groups to corral schools of fish, then exploding skyward through the mass, mouths wide open. By July the eaglets are on the wing, and they spend their days practising landings on bare branches near their nests. By *Kayitsapakplth*, the "salal berry moon" of August, the first of the shorebirds appear on the beaches on their way south, their short Arctic breeding season having come to an end. The bears have moved inland, following the cycle of berries as different varieties become ripe: salmonberries, then huckleberries, then salal and finally, by September and October, cinnamock. On shore, humans enjoy the treats of the season: barbecued coho salmon, fresh boiled Dungeness crab and wild berry pie.

Bald eagles are common on West Coast shores.

Humpback whales, once hunted to near-extinction, are now regular summer visitors along the outer coast. **John Forde**

Autumn carries a special energy: the culmination of the breeding, the feeding, the growing, the pollinating—all of the procreating and nurturing that the plants and animals have engaged in throughout the spring and summer. Young have been raised and instructed in the ways of the world, seeds have been set to the wind. Many animals prepare to leave. The gray whales and humpbacks head off to winter breeding grounds. Hummingbirds flit through the trees, gleaning their last drops of energy from tiny blossoms to sustain them for the long journey south. Salmon, having spent two to seven years in the open ocean, return to the streams of their birth to perform the final and most significant act of their lives: to spawn, laying the eggs that ensure the survival of their race. Bears prepare for the stillness of winter by fattening up. They congregate at the salmon streams, where for a short time each year a major food source is nearby and accessible. Dragging the dying fish into the forest and chewing on them as their life ebbs away, the bears leave the remains on the forest floor, an important fertilizer that ensures the continuing health of the rain forest.

In the villages, the locals breathe a sigh of relief. Although they depend upon

A chum salmon passes carcasses of earlier spawners as it enters the stream of its birth to spawn on Meares Island.

visitors for much of their communities' income, the crazy months of summer are exhausting. As the tourists thin out, the locals can take a few days off, catch up on the friendships that were neglected over the summer and begin to make plans for the quiet months to come. Some will have work through the slower winter season, but many will head south in search of sunshine or surf.

In the Nuu-chah-nulth villages, autumn is a busy time. For millennia, this has been the time to gather and store foods for the coming winter. Tribal councils contract fishing boats to deliver thousands of salmon to the communities. When the call comes in on the radio that the boat is on its way, dozens of villagers descend to the dock. There they clean the fish, the young people using knives and the elders using their traditional cutting tool, the *chih-tooklh*. Smokehouses are fired up and space is cleared in the freezers. Pressure cookers for canning are dusted off. Fish heads and spines are chucked straight into the pot for soup. Meanwhile, children are sent out to gather salal berries and blackberries, which will be made into jam or frozen for pies.

Ahousaht elder Rosie Swan uses the traditional *chih-tooklh* knife to clean her salmon.

A black bear lands a salmon at Thornton Creek near Ucluelet.

Following pages: A winter sun sets behind Frank Island, Chesterman Beach.

By the start of winter, all of the residents—human and animal—have either headed south or laid down enough stores of food or fat to survive the cold, dark months to come, especially the January moon of *Wiyaqhamilth* ("no food-getting for a long time").

Winter on the coast has a compelling intensity, a contradictory blend of peacefulness and fury. Days are short and dark. Foul weather can last for weeks, with violent windstorms powering horizontal driving rain and battering the coast with huge ocean swells 10 or 15 metres high. Thunderous waves hurl themselves at the shore, tossing giant driftwood logs like toothpicks high and dry upon the shoreline. Between storms come fleeting moments of brightness and calm, as the sky breaks abruptly for a few hours or even a few days and the sun emerges. Suddenly the wild West Coast seems a paradise, while the rest of the country remains locked in the icy clutches of northern winter.

Even during the harshest storms, the rain forest floor remains a place of calm, sheltered from the fury of winter as the treetops above sway and groan. Most of the songbirds leave for the season, and the few who remain dart secretively through the undergrowth. Diving ducks and trumpeter swans frequent the quiet waters of sheltered inlets. Temperatures on the coast remain mild throughout the winter, and most years the snowfall in lower areas is light; many animals, such as the tree frogs and the bears, do not fully hibernate, but fall into

Youngster dons winter beachwear while West Coast surfers brave strong winds and even snow.

a light semi-hibernation, emerging on warmer days to scrounge around for food. Winter is also an important food-gathering time for Native people, who keep an eye on the weather, digging for clams when the tides are low and the weather is fine, and hunting ducks up the sheltered inlets when storms approach.

The storm clouds that drop so much rain on the coast blast inland, rising up the mountainsides. Up in the high country, swirling blizzards coat the rugged peaks in snow. The moisture stored here will feed the lush forests below over the coming year.

For the human communities of the West Coast, the fury of the winter storms serves as a forceful reminder of how frail we humans are in the face of nature. Our mobility is curtailed in many ways. Strong winds keep boats at their docks; snowstorms at Sutton Pass cut off our only road access to the outside world; low fog and cloud keep aircraft from flying. Power outages are frequent. The locals who haven't headed south resign themselves to a long, dark season of seemingly endless potluck dinners and yoga classes. Gumboots and rubber outerwear are *de rigueur* and considered acceptable even at the occasional formal gathering, but all plans are flexible and weather-dependent. Winter is a quiet, social time for us, a time when the deep bonds of friendship in a small and remote community are reaffirmed.

For months, the angry grey skies and driving rain seem to continue without cease. Then one day the sky opens and the sun breathes warmth on the land again. The skunk cabbage pokes up through the mud and the frogs start their song.

Rocky outcrops off Chesterman Beach offer good storm-watching, but watch out for those rogue waves.

2 In the Beginning

THE CENTRAL COAST OF
VANCOUVER ISLAND
IS A ZONE OF DYNAMIC
CONFLICT BETWEEN POWERFUL
FORCES. THE MEETING OF THE
COLOSSAL LAND MASS OF THE
NORTH AMERICAN CONTINENT
WITH THE VAST PACIFIC
OCEAN AFFECTS PATTERNS OF
ATMOSPHERIC CIRCULATION
AND OCEAN CURRENTS. ABRUPT
TEMPERATURE GRADIENTS AND
HIGH MOUNTAIN RANGES
DEFLECT MASSES OF AIR FROM
THEIR COURSE, SPITTING OUT
ANGRY SWIRLS OF CLOUD AND
GENERATING INTENSE STORMS.

Lennard Island pounded by winter
storm swell.

Ice age effects: glacial till (top), high, jagged peaks that escaped glacial erosion (middle), striations incised into bedrock by passing ice sheets (bottom).

The storm waves claw away at the coastline, drawing pieces of the mighty continent back into the sea where it formed.

Wind, surf and shore are not the only elements that contend at this wild edge. The twisted rock formations and scooped-out inlets bear witness to a past of even greater dynamism: volcanic eruptions, unimaginably huge ice sheets, and inundations and regressions of the sea. For this is not just a point of division between land and sea, but a point of collision between some of the planet's fundamental building blocks.

THE MAKING OF THE LAND

Hundreds of millions of years ago, the North American continent was much smaller than it is today. Its western shore was somewhere around where Calgary is now. Through the slow geologic process of subduction, the tectonic plate that underlies the Pacific Ocean slid steadily eastward, forcing its way under the lighter continental plate. Over millions of years, volcanic island chains carried on top of the oceanic plate collided with the continent. The immense force of the collisions uplifted the curving spine of mountains that winds its way down the entire west coast of the Americas. The volcanic islands themselves fused to the continent, building the coast farther out to the west with each collision.

Most of Vancouver Island, as well as the areas of Haida Gwaii and the mainland around Vancouver, formed when dinosaurs still dominated the Earth, from an island chain that hit the coast 100 million years ago. This giant twisted mass of rock—made of volcanic lavas, granite, sandstone and limestone—is known to geologists as *Wrangellia*.

The final major tectonic collision occurred around 55 million years ago, just after the end of the dinosaur age. Mudstone and sandstone from the sea floor were plastered to the outermost coast, forming what is known as the *Pacific Rim Terrane*. These rocks form a thin strip along the coast all the way from Tofino to Ucluelet. Beach-goers who have marvelled at the twisted black outcroppings that punctuate the sandy shoreline, perhaps mistaking them for basaltic lava, have actually been admiring terrane-borne mudstone. Pressure between the plates still causes faulting, earthquake activity and tilting of the land; while the west coast of Vancouver Island is rising due to this tectonic pressure, the east coast is subsiding as the island tilts. Subduction is not a smooth process. Friction between the subducting plate and the overriding plate can make the plates get stuck, building up tectonic pressure. This intense pressure makes the Tofino–Ucluelet area rise about one millimetre each year, and pushes it northeastward at a rate of more than one centimetre per year. In geological terms, that is very fast!

Every few hundred years the pressure builds to the breaking point, and the West Coast pops back out like a spring, shifting up to five metres westward and a metre downward. This kind of earthquake, called a *megathrust earthquake*, only occurs along subduction zones and is the strongest kind of earthquake in the world. For several minutes the ground shakes intensely, swaying back and forth, leaving almost nothing standing. Often it is followed within an hour or two by a tsunami, or tidal wave. Here in the Pacific Northwest, these earthquakes occur about once every 500 years. That is just an average, though: some have struck as close together as 200 years. By an amazing sequence of detective work using carbon dating of plant matter cross-referenced against growth rings of trees and tsunami records from Japan, scientists have determined that the last megathrust earthquake here occurred at about 9:00 p.m. local time, on January 26, 1700.

The Nuu-chah-nulth people have many stories of the ground shaking and of great floods, some of which may have been tsunamis. Although most of these are not dated, the Pachena Bay people just south of Barkley Sound tell of a coastal village where the land started shaking in the middle of the night, and then sank so quickly that no one could escape. Everyone in the village drowned. It is quite possible that this story records the 1700 earthquake and subsequent tsunami.

THE ICE AGE

All of the geological events that formed the land mass that is now Vancouver Island took place many millions of years ago. The sculpting of the land into the familiar mountaintops and valleys of today happened much more recently— within the last few tens of thousands of years. The mighty glaciers of the last ice age, which reached its peak 17,000 years ago, are responsible for this artistry. The

Island's highest mountain peaks protruded above the ice sheets, and they are still rugged and pointy, having escaped the erosive effects of the glaciers. The smaller mountains, such as 730-metre Lone Cone opposite Tofino on Meares Island, have been rounded by the moving ice. They give us an idea of the great thickness of the ice sheets. So much water was tied up in ice that the world's ocean levels went down by over 100 metres. In some places the weight of the ice made the land sink as well, causing much local variation in sea level.

At lower elevations, glacial striations in smoothly polished rock surfaces also bear testimony to the movement of the glaciers as they slowly ground their way down river valleys, gouging out the watersheds and salt-water inlets of today. On many outer coastal beaches, colourful rounded boulders rest upon the uniform black bedrock, sticking out like so many sore thumbs. Known as *glacial erratics*, these exotic stones were transported from distant locales by the moving ice sheets. The glaciers also left beds of fine grey clay, settled out of the huge glacial lakes that formed behind dams of ice, and mounds of glacial till, a coarse mixture of clay, sand, gravel and

Having worked for many years as a geologist, I learned to study outcrops like this one for clues to ages past. **Meg Stewart**

Tla-o-qui-aht Gisele
Martin strips cedar bark,
which she might make
into baskets, hats and
rope.

pebbles. Inland, the till is overgrown by the tangle of rainforest vegetation; on the coast, thousands of years of wave action has sorted the till into its constituent parts, washed away the fine clays and thrown back the light sands, forming the region's spectacular ocean beaches.

When the Cordilleran ice sheet started to retreat about 14,000 years ago, the first parts to melt were the edges of the sheet, at the shorelines. Land areas appeared suddenly around the coasts. Plant seeds were blown in by the wind from nearby refugia, areas that had remained ice-free. Insects, birds and animals soon followed. Bit by bit, mosses, grasses and sedges colonized the rocky hills and the clay- and gravel-filled lowlands left bare by the melting ice. As the vegetation mat built up and the climate slowly warmed, shrubs and eventually trees arrived. A forest started to rise. Pine and spruce came first, and by 7,000 years ago, Douglas fir was growing. It was only 4,000 years ago that western red cedar became abundant.

It is not known for certain when salmon appeared in the rivers on Vancouver Island. They arrived in waters farther north only about 6,000 years ago, but they probably were moving up Vancouver Island's rivers well before that. The salmon would have been followed closely by black bears. As the forest gradually matured and animals like deer, marten, raccoon and birds arrived, the complex ecosystem of the coastal temperate rain forest slowly evolved.

"Exotic" boulders, different in composition from local bedrock, were carried from afar by glaciers.

THE FIRST HUMANS

Until recently, many archaeologists thought that all First Nations people arrived in North America on foot about 11,000 years ago, when the retreating ice and lowered sea level left a land bridge between Alaska and Siberia. Archaeological discoveries have now shown that the settlement of the Americas was far more complex than a single pulse of hunters following mammoths over a land bridge. While the full story has yet to be revealed, it appears likely that there was, among other things, at least one significant migration of a maritime culture—seafood-dependent people who travelled in canoes or rafts—*before* the end of the ice age. These people may have been ancestors of the West Coast indigenous people, including the Nuu-chah-nulth. However they arrived, the people known today as the Nuu-chah-nulth are part of a cultural group that historically occupied the territory from Neah Bay in Washington state northward along the outer coast of Vancouver Island as far as the Brooks Peninsula. Traditionally these groups did not have an overall name for themselves because they were not politically unified. They existed as many small, separate tribes linked by common language, culture and family ties. For 200 years they were referred to collectively as the "Nootka" people, a name mistakenly given them by Captain James Cook in 1778. *Nuu-chah-nulth*, which means "all along the mountains," was chosen as the official replacement for *Nootka* by the Nuu-chah-nulth Tribal Council in 1980.

The name of each Nuu-chah-nulth tribe ends with the suffix *aht*. Pronounced with a breathy sigh, *aht* means "the people of . . ." For example, the Toquaht are the people of the village called T'ukw'aa ("the narrow beach"), and the Ahousaht are from Ahous ("the bay with its back toward the sun"). The Tla-o-qui-aht are the people who are *tla-ook*, "different": they originate from the inland areas around Clayoquot Lake, unlike their outer coastal cousins.

Six tribes occupy what is now known as Barkley Sound: Hupacasath (sometimes spelled Opetchesaht), Tseshaht, Uchucklesaht, Huu-ay-aht, Toquaht and Ucluelet. Clayoquot Sound is the traditional territory of three tribes: Tla-o-qui-aht, Ahousaht and Hesquiaht. (When spelling place names the final "h" is dropped, as in "Ahousat.")

The ancestors of the Nuu-chah-nulth likely arrived here on the coast not long after the end of the ice age, and probably brought many of their maritime survival skills with them. As cedar and salmon returned to the coast, the wealth that these two resources provided would have allowed Native culture to advance even further.

Western red cedar trees, immense, plentiful and easily worked, were sources of shelter, transport and clothing. Huge cedar logs provided the framework of massive longhouses clad with broad cedar planks. Dugout canoes carved out of single cedar logs were used for voyaging, fishing, hunting sea mammals and making war. Cedar bark was also an important resource: it was twisted into strong rope or woven into baskets, capes, skirts and hats. Salmon were the lifeblood of the Native cultures. Abundant harvests of spawning salmon could be smoked and dried for sustenance year-round. This staple, augmented by such secondary foods as herring, shellfish, whales, deer, elk and many plant foods, left the West Coast tribes with enough leisure time to spend on cultural pursuits such as fine carving, storytelling and elaborate winter ceremonials.

The Nuu-chah-nulth migrated between "outside" and "inside" village sites, leaving

their longhouse frames standing, but carrying with them the outer house planks as well as their household goods and stored food. This migration followed the main seasonal food sources, and spring, summer and fall were busy times for gathering and preserving foods. The winter village sites were chosen for protection from the storms that lash the coast.

The territory of each tribe was clearly defined. Tribal groups were small, and a territory was often centred upon a valued resource, such as the mouth of a productive salmon stream or a sheltered cove with a lookout point that served as a base for hunting whales. Tribes traded with each other for the goods that they could not produce in sufficient quantity on their own land, and in this way commodities travelled great distances up and down the coast. Eulachon grease and walrus tusks came down from the Far North, and camas tubers arrived from Salish territory to the south.

EXPLORERS

Archaeological digs at Nootka and in Barkley Sound reveal that West Coast life went on with little material change for more than 4,000 years before the coming of Europeans. While there were skirmishes and even intertribal wars over territory, in general a stable society with a well-defined culture endured in a state of equilibrium. This changed forever in August 1774, when the 26-metre Spanish frigate *Santiago* under the command of Juan Pérez made contact with Natives near Hesquiat. Pérez had been dispatched from San Blas by the viceroy of Mexico to investigate the threat of southward expansion by the Russians, who were established in Alaska. He was instructed to remove Indians "from the shadow of idolatry" and to be on the lookout for trade items such as gold, silver, pepper, cloves, cinnamon, nutmeg, wheat, corn and chickpeas. Although none of the Spaniards went ashore, gifts were exchanged, and one of the Natives reputedly stole two Spanish silver spoons from the ship. Life on the coast resumed with the Spaniards' departure, and for four years continued as it had for centuries. Then, in the spring of 1778, Captain James Cook sailed across the Pacific Ocean into Nootka Sound, the next major inlet north of Clayoquot Sound.

Pleasantly surprised to find himself in a safe harbour and encountering friendly Natives, Cook eventually gave the name of Friendly Cove to their settlement (already known to the Mowachaht tribe as Yuquot). He and his crew ended up staying for a month, mingling happily with the Natives. Cook and his men befriended the powerful Chief Maquinna, traded with the Mowachaht, fished, gathered feed for

Trade beads dating from early 1800s link the anchor recently found near Tofino to the storied *Tonquin* disaster of 1811.

shipboard cattle and brewed spruce beer to prevent scurvy. The writings of Cook and his crew have provided us with much of the information we have on West Coast culture prior to European contact.

Captain Cook was killed in Hawaii less than a year after his visit to Nootka. However, subsequent reports by his crew of this newly "discovered" territory, especially the fact that sea otter skins could be acquired from the Natives for trinkets and sold for grand profits in China, ensured that many other ships would soon arrive.

The British activity aroused concern among the Spanish, who claimed sovereignty over the entire Northwest Coast, and in 1789 the viceroy of Mexico dispatched two ships under Esteban José Martínez to consolidate Spain's claim to Vancouver Island by building a fort at Nootka. Conflicts with British traders soon escalated into an international incident known as the Nootka Controversy, and England and Spain came to the brink of war. At the centre of the dispute were the two Spanish silver spoons, which Captain Cook later found a Native man wearing around his neck. Spain claimed that the presence of the two spoons among the Nootka people proved that they had discovered the region first; Britain dismissed this claim and hung its hat on Cook's more substantial exploration. Eventually Britain prevailed, and in 1795 the Spanish garrison, the first European settlement on Vancouver Island, was abandoned.

Within a decade of the first white man setting foot on the shores of Vancouver Island, the West Coast became a virtual thoroughfare for trading ships hungry for otter pelts. Relations between the traders and the Natives were friendly at first, but soon soured. In 1791 the American Captain Robert Gray burnt the Tla-o-qui-aht village of Opitsat to the ground, destroying forever its finely carved longhouses. In 1803 the Mowachaht captured the American ship *Boston* in Nootka Sound, taking two sailors captive and killing the rest. In 1811 the Tla-o-qui-aht attacked the American ship *Tonquin*, in part in revenge for the destruction of Opitsat two decades before. They killed all but one of the crew, but lost several hundred of their own when a wounded crewman detonated the powder magazine.

The destruction of the *Tonquin* was a significant blow to white–Native relations, and for nearly 50 years both European and American ships avoided the West Coast and its people. The sea otter had been hunted to near extinction anyway. But by the 1860s, traders and settlers started to trickle back into the region, attracted by a new demand for fur seal pelts. Around that time, trading posts were established in Spring Cove (at the entrance to Barkley Sound) and at Clayoquot (on Stubbs Island), just inside the southern entrance to Clayoquot Sound. These two trading posts are the original settlements that, through time, eventually became the foundations for the communities of Ucluelet and Tofino.

After hunting the sea otter to near extinction, the maritime fur trade turned its attention to the fur seal.

3
The Road to Ucluelet

M OST OF THE MILLION VISITORS WHO HEAD TO THE PACIFIC RIM EACH YEAR TRAVEL BY ROAD. BY *THE* ROAD. THE WHOLE JOURNEY IS, IN LOCAL PARLANCE, A PROGRESSION OF "THE'S": *THE* ROAD, *THE* PASS AND FINALLY *THE* JUNCTION.

The clear, fresh waters and sandy beaches of Kennedy Lake make it one of the region's favoured bathing areas.

For those of us who live on the outer coast, the road, Highway 4, is our lifeline, the single thread that connects us to the outside world. The isolation is palpable—even on the best of days it is a long, winding drive across the island. In the raging furor of West Coast winter, even this thread may break. Then nothing gets in or out.

When I have been away, I always feel a surge of excitement as I step off the ferry at Nanaimo and head north up the highway, just from knowing I am back on my beloved island. From the Island Highway at Qualicum Beach, Highway 4 heads west, a narrow, twisting route that hugs steep, forested slopes. We start immediately to climb, passing through the towering Douglas firs of Cathedral Grove. When we arrive at Port Alberni Summit, which at 375 metres above sea level is the island equivalent of the Continental Divide, I feel even closer to home; from this point on the rivers flow west to the open Pacific coast. From here we descend rapidly back to sea level at Port Alberni.

Although barely a third of the way across the island, this town at the head of Alberni Inlet is technically on the West Coast. Traditionally the home of the Tseshaht people, Port Alberni got going in earnest as a European settlement in 1860, when Captain Edward Stamp, an entrepreneurial English shipmaster, selected it as the location for BC's first large export sawmill. That mill failed a few years later, as did an attempt to found BC's first paper mill in 1894, but Port Alberni's fate as a lumbering centre was sealed. More mills appeared as steam-powered logging methods made it possible to reach deeper into the forest, and in 1946 Bloedel, Stewart and Welch built a pulp mill that eventually developed into one of the largest in Canada. Fed by forest industry revenues, Port Alberni grew into a city of 18,000 people by the 1990s, by far

Sutton Pass, elevation 175 metres, marks the height of land between Barkley Sound and Clayoquot Sound.

the largest on the West Coast, but in recent years it has suffered the fate of many one-industry towns as forest industry activity declined and the local economy tanked. Port Alberni wasn't built for beauty, but it has an interesting working waterfront, a decent museum and a fun display of old logging machines in the dockside train station, where a real steam train runs out to a restored steam sawmill in summer—but don't look for an explanation of why so much of the region's lumbering activity is now relegated to museum displays. Like many BC coast timber towns, Port Alberni is still in official denial about its role in depleting the forest resource.

Barkley Sound is a broad bite out of Vancouver Island's west coast. Its mouth is dotted by a cluster of forested islets called the Broken Group. At its southern entrance are Cape Beale lighthouse and the village of Bamfield, and at its northern entrance the lighthouse at Amphitrite Point keeps watch over the village of Ucluelet. Farther out in the Sound, a scattering of larger islands forms the Deer Group. Beyond the isles, the waters narrow to a steep-sided fjord, Alberni Inlet, which twists its way 50 kilometres into the heart of Vancouver Island.

The towering Douglas firs of Cathedral Grove stand as a reminder of what has been taken from this landscape.

From Port Alberni the road follows the shores of Sproat Lake, then starts a meandering climb to Sutton Pass, the drainage divide between Barkley Sound and Clayoquot Sound. Sutton Pass is *the* Pass, and at times *the* barrier to communication between our communities and the outside world. At only 175 metres, it does not seem significantly high, but it is the first obstruction for moisture-laden clouds blowing in from the Pacific. In summer it is often the boundary between sunshine and warmth on the Alberni side and blustering rain and fog on the Clayoquot side. In winter, snowdrifts several metres high pile up on the roadsides, and raging blizzards produce white-out conditions that keep tow-truck drivers busy.

As we descend from the Pass, the vegetation changes subtly but significantly. Flowering dogwood and arbutus, those arresting trees with their peeling coppery bark and bright evergreen leaves, both disappear, and Douglas fir is less abundant. The forest becomes more lush, more darkly green, more impenetrable and mysterious. This is the coastal temperate rain forest. I am home.

One of the defining characteristics of the true rain forest is, not surprisingly, the high amount of rainfall it receives. On average, about 2.5 metres of precipitation falls on the west coast of Vancouver Island each year, more than double that of nearby Nanaimo. Another characteristic of the rain forest here on the soggy side of the island is that the precipitation is spread throughout the year. Although there is less moisture in summer, there is no period of sustained drought. There is less danger of fire here than on the drier east coast, where catastrophic forest fires ravage the landscape every few centuries. The wet West Coast rain forest, by contrast, just keeps growing—although periodic windstorms fray it around the edges a little. Individual trees die and are replaced one at a time, but the plant community itself continues to grow and become more complex, in an unbroken timeline that may go back thousands of years.

The forest structure is layered, starting with the upper canopy of dominant conifers, principally western hemlock and western red cedar, then moving down to the understory layer of smaller trees, then the shrub layer, and finally the spongy, mossy forest floor, where a universe of micro-organisms resides. These organisms, particularly the fungal networks called mycorrhizae, are crucial to forest health.

Trees of many sizes and ages grow together in the mature rain forest, their branches festooned with epiphytic plants, dangling fronds of lichens and exuberant trusses of

Opposite: The upper Kennedy River threads its way through a picturesque canyon.

These slender second-growth trees will be re-logged long before they attain the girth of the first-growth stumps of their predecessors.

Highway 4 winds along-
side Kennedy Lake for
15 km.

fern. The biomass or weight of living matter in these forests, estimated to be between 500 and 2,000 metric tons per hectare, exceeds that of tropical rain forests, making the temperate rain forest the heavyweight champion of all the earth's ecosystems.

Unfortunately, much of the ancient rain forest along Highway 4 is gone. East of Port Alberni, only the isolated 136-hectare remnant of old growth at Cathedral Grove remains to give the traveller a hint as to what has been taken from this landscape. This stand of giant Douglas firs, mixed with western red cedar and western hemlock, was donated to the province by the H.R. MacMillan Export Company in 1944, and is now preserved as MacMillan Provincial Park. Although officially protected, this orphaned colony of ancient trees is surrounded by clear-cuts and exposed to winter storms, one of which blew down about 10 percent of its ancient firs in January 1997.

The Alberni Valley and surrounding lands for miles in all directions have been extensively logged over the past 140 years. Industry spokesmen such as Patrick Moore argue that the forest rapidly recovers after clear-cutting and regains the full spectrum of associated life forms or biodiversity. But if you look out the window at the trees as you travel along the shore of Sproat Lake, your own eyes will tell you in an instant that this second-growth forest is nothing like Cathedral Grove or the pristine rain forest we will have a chance to visit later on Meares Island. Nor will the so-called managed forest ever fully regain the wondrous complexity and mass of its old-growth predecessor, because it will be cut down again while still in its youth, and this accelerated cycle of planting and harvesting will go on endlessly—unless the ecosystem collapses from soil exhaustion, plagues or over-stress, as has happened elsewhere.

The Wet West Coast

The average amount of precipitation on the West Coast is relatively high at 2.5 metres per year. However, certain valleys form microclimates that get even more rain. Tofino receives an average of 3.3 metres. The wettest place in Canada is Henderson Lake, just in from Barkley Sound's northern shore. One year it received more than 8 metres of rainfall. The record for the most rainfall in one day is held by Ucluelet, which measured 489 millimetres of rain—nearly half a metre—in one day!

The road follows the winding Kennedy River through a valley scooped out by glaciers during the last ice age. Smooth glaciated rock faces hang above, and the river rushes and tumbles below. Hairpin turns leave little room for error. During rainstorms, the rock faces turn into instant waterfalls that splatter onto the traffic. In a final flurry of twists and curves, the road descends to the shores of Kennedy Lake for the last meandering stretch through the rain forest to the junction: turn right for Tofino, left for Ucluelet.

The Kennedy River system is home to an important sockeye salmon run. From Kennedy Lake, the lower Kennedy River debouches into the salt waters of Clayoquot Sound about 20 kilometres up Tofino Inlet from the village of Tofino. The little bay at the river mouth is still known as Cannery Bay, after the fish cannery that operated there from the late 1800s until 1931, when falling salmon prices forced it to close.

For millennia, the rich and reliable returns of salmon to the rivers provided the Nuu-chah-nulth people with a dependable food source. Salmon also played a crucial role for the first non-Native inhabitants of the West Coast. With the arrival

Above: Chum salmon take on an increasingly grotesque appearance as they approach their Clayoquot spawning beds.

Left: Vista up Clayoquot Arm, the northern branch of sprawling Kennedy Lake.

of the Japanese in the 1920s, more efficient methods of fishing were brought to the coast, and the fishing industry grew in prominence. Ten canneries sprung up along the coast, providing employment to settlers and Natives. By 1962 there was a fleet of 1,000 boats, mainly trollers, operating out of Bamfield, Port Alberni, Ucluelet, Tofino, Nootka, Kyuquot and Winter Harbour. Each community acquired fish processing and supply facilities to service the trade. Salmon became the West Coast currency.

One Vancouver resident who grew up in Ucluelet in the 1960s spoke of the abundance of salmon: "Our house was by the dock. The fishermen used to leave the smaller fish on the dock and we would just pick them up and take them home. I was shocked when I moved to Vancouver and found we had to *pay* for salmon! I always thought it was *free!*"

Six species of salmon (*Oncorhyncus* spp.) are native to the Pacific coast of North America: chum, pink, coho, sockeye, chinook and steelhead. Salmon are anadromous fish, which means they reproduce in fresh water and the juveniles then migrate to the sea to mature. After several years at sea, they return to the streams and rivers of their birth and lay their eggs in the heart of the coastal temperate rain forest.

The old-growth rain forest is essential to the survival of young salmon. Fallen

The MV *Lady Rose*, last of the old-time coasters, plies the waters of Barkley Sound.

mossy logs help to create quiet pools in which the salmon fry live; the rainforest canopy provides shade, moderating the temperature of the pools and streams; the cool forest retains moisture so that streams do not dry up over the summer. In a twist that is typical of the intricate web of relationships in nature, salmon also help to nourish the forest: their spawned-out carcasses are spread throughout the watershed by bears and other predators. Studies in Clayoquot Sound show that this natural fish fertilizer provides as much as 75 percent of the nitrogen in some trees.

The annual salmon migration never fails to move me. No one could have prepared me for the emotion I felt the first time I witnessed these large fish writhing in the shallow waters during the final moments of their lives. Riddled with gashes, infection and great patches of fungus, they still had enough spirit to battle their way up waterfalls and excavate metre-wide nests in coarse gravel to lay their eggs and perpetuate their race. The Kennedy River and Thornton Creek hatchery near Ucluelet are two easily accessible sites where this miracle can be witnessed. Bears frequent both sites during the spawn, focussing so intently on the fish that they barely glance at human observers.

The Kennedy River system lies within the traditional territory of the Tla-o-qui-aht. To the south, Barkley Sound was once home to dozens of small tribes. After they were depopulated by disease and warfare, some of these small tribes became extinct over the last century and a half, and others amalgamated. Now, six Nuu-chah-nulth tribes claim territory in Barkley Sound: the Ucluelet and Toquaht at the northern entrance to the Sound, the Tseshaht in the Broken Islands and in part of Alberni Inlet, the Huu-ay-aht along the Sound's southeastern shore, the Uchucklesaht at the bottom of Alberni Inlet and the Hupacasath (Opetchesaht) at the top of Alberni Inlet.

During the 1840s, only a few years before the arrival of the first settlers, the Ucluelet and Toquaht engaged in the Long War. The Ucluelet opened hostilities over a missing slave. The Toquaht formed an alliance with other local tribes, including the Tsesaht and Huu-ay-aht, and mounted a counterattack. The war ended when the Ucluelet moved into Toquaht territory, and significant numbers of Toquaht were killed.

Since the Long War, tribal territories have remained fairly constant and well defined. The Ucluelet's main village is Itatsoo, across the inlet from the town of Ucluelet. The Huu-ay-aht village of Anacla is just outside of Bamfield, at the southern entrance to Barkley Sound. The principal Toquaht village is Macoah, near Toquart Bay in northern Barkley Sound, although many of the band members live in or near Ucluelet. The Hupacasath village of Ahahswinis, near the mouth of the Somass River, lies within the present limits of Port Alberni, and just past it along the highway is the Tseshaht village of Tsahaheh. The small isolated Uchucklesaht village of Kildonan lies to the south of Port Alberni, but many of its members reside in Port Alberni town.

Although each tribe maintains one main village site, in Barkley Sound almost any sheltered beach or river mouth shows signs of habitation from within the last one or two thousand years. Dr. Alan McMillan has spent three decades boating around Barkley Sound excavating these "younger" sites, but finding signs of older occupation proved more difficult. McMillan knew that the Nuu-chah-nulth stayed close to the water, and that 4,000 years ago sea level was about 4 metres higher than it is now, so he set about looking for a higher site behind the ancient Tseshaht village of Ts'ishaa, on Benson Island in the Broken Group. He excavated a ridge in the forest and obtained materials that, when carbon dated, showed that people were living at Ts'ishaa 5,000 years ago. So far, this is the oldest evidence of human occupation within Nuu-chah-nulth territory. People were undoubtedly living here even earlier, but during that period sea level was lower than it is now, so any archaeological remains would have washed away.

One of the better records of Native life in the early stages of European contact is found in *Scenes and Studies of Savage Life* (1868) by Gilbert Malcolm Sproat. In the summer of 1860, Sproat arrived at the top of Alberni Inlet, where Port Alberni now stands, to help Captain Stamp build his mill. The site, which Stamp had purchased from the government, was occupied by the Tseshaht village of Nuupts'ikapis. Twenty pounds' worth of trade goods coupled with a show of force from the ships' cannons convinced the Tseshaht to relocate up the Somass River, but the words of their chief accurately foretold the dark events that would occur over the following century: "We see your ships, and hear things that make our hearts grow faint. They say that more King George men will soon be here, and will take our land, our firewood, our fishing grounds; that we shall be placed on a little spot, and shall have to do everything

Gem-like islets make the Broken Group in Barkley Sound a sea kayaker's paradise.

according to the fancies of the King George men . . . We do not wish to sell our land nor our water; let your friends stay in their own country."

In 1874 the national Parliament passed the Indian Act, making Native people legal wards of the state and confining them to reserve lands. Christian missions and residential schools were established. Families were fragmented and oral history links that maintained knowledge born of millennia were broken. But by far the worst of the misfortunes were caused by introduced diseases. In the 1770s and early 1780s, only a few years after Captain Cook's arrival, Ditidaht and Salish tribes on southern Vancouver Island had been hit by smallpox epidemics. Throughout the 1800s, smallpox caused waves of death, significantly depleting Nuu-chah-nulth populations. Tuberculosis, measles and sexually transmitted diseases also took their toll. Estimates of the Native population prior to European contact vary; the Nuu-chah-nulth people (including Ditidaht and Makah) numbered between 10,000 and 31,000. By 1885 the Nuu-chah-nulth–Ditidaht population was 3,500, and by 1939 it was down to only 1,605 survivors. Today the Nuu-chah-nulth population is growing again as they struggle to recover from more than a century of abuse and loss, to regain their rights and to fight the cycles of violence and addiction that ravage their communities.

The town of Ucluelet is the principal settlement on Barkley Sound's north shore. It

The storm-tossed mouth of Barkley Sound, viewed from Ucluelet's Wild Pacific Trail.

Right: Beachcombed fishing floats dangle from a deck.

is a small village situated on the narrow Ucluth Peninsula, bordered on the west by surf-pounded beaches and on the east by the calm waters of Ucluelet Inlet. Ucluelet, which means "people with the safe landing place," owes its existence to its fine harbour and its strong ties to the sea. In the early 20th century, it was home port to a fleet of more than a hundred small West Coast salmon trollers. Many of these were owned by residents of Japanese descent who were interned during World War II, a circumstance that devastated the fleet. Like Bamfield and Tofino, Ucluelet had a lifeboat rescue station, and maritime disasters loom large in local lore. The leading landmark is the Amphitrite Point Light Station, which Ucluelet proudly advertises as the only lighthouse on the Pacific Rim that visitors can drive up to in the family car. Unfortunately, its bunker-like tower makes Amphitrite one of the coast's less romantic beacons, but guarding over the busiest small boat harbour on the outer coast and co-ordinating the rescue work of the local lifeboat made it one of the more active lights over the years. The town's maritime heritage lingers on in its famous floating hotel, the *Canadian Princess*, and in the driftwood and fishing floats that decorate village yards. No home is far from the sea, and many families own a boat of some kind. Weather is an unfailing topic of conversation.

Driftwood decor emphasizes Ucluelet's seaside ambience.

Ucluelet evolved from several smaller settlements. During the 1860s, a fur-trading post was founded by Captain Peter Francis, a sealer, at Spring Cove on the extreme tip of the Ucluth Peninsula. In 1861 the Sutton brothers established a sawmill and store at Port Albion, on the inland side of the inlet where the Native village of Itatsoo and a Presbyterian mission and church were located. The renowned BC painter Emily Carr visited Itatsoo in 1898, and recorded the presence of "large, squat houses made of thick, hand hewn cedar planks, pegged and slotted together. The side walls were made of driftwood. Bark and shakes weighted with stones against the wind, were used for roofs. Every house stood separate from the next. Wind roared through the narrow spaces between. Houses and people were alike. Wind, rain, forest and sea had done the same things to both—both were soaked through and through with sunshine, too." In 1937 the old mill was converted to a processing plant for pilchards, and a cannery was added during World War II, accompanied by a fleet of big seine boats. For a while Port Albion, or "Ucluelet East," was a booming community with its own school, but today the east side of the inlet is mostly quiet except for the Itatsoo reserve. Around the turn of the 19th century, settlers cleared farms around the inlet shore and a small settlement called Stapleby was established at the head of the inlet but it is now long gone.

Following pages: Foaming reefs surround the town of Ucluelet, built around the safe harbour of Ucluelet Inlet.

In 1900, gold was discovered in the beach sands of Wreck Bay, now known as Florencia Bay. According to the census taken in the following year, 105 people lived

Above: The 80-metre *Canadian Princess*, a floating resort, restaurant and landmark in Ucluelet.

Right: Ukee Days logger sports contestant works up a sweat in the springboard chop event.

in the area and half of them listed their occupation as "miner." This gold rush started Ucluelet's roller-coaster ride as a boom-and-bust resource town. Storms damaged the mining equipment repeatedly and the richest gold soon ran out. Fur trading was still an important industry, but through the early part of the century Ucluelet thrived mainly as a fishing centre. Then, in the 1930s, salmon prices collapsed. Ucluelet was an important seaplane base during World War II, but then the war ended. Fishing rebounded, but by the 1950s logging began to dominate the local economy.

For much of this time, Ucluelet's only access to the outside world was by sea. From 1913 to 1952, the steamship *Princess Maquinna* arrived from Victoria every 10 days. There was also regular boat service to Port Alberni, starting in 1913 with the 10-metre MV *Tofino*. In 1960 the MV *Lady Rose* took over the run, and she still plies these waters today. A road that connected Ucluelet to Tofino, so that travellers no longer had to time their trip with the tides in order to drive across miles of treacherous beach, was finally completed in the 1940s, but that road brought them no closer to the outside world. For decades residents had muttered about a link to civilization and finally, in 1954, two logging companies agreed to link their existing roads, connecting the west

coast with Port Alberni. This road, a twisting, gravelled, potholed affair riddled with switchbacks, was completed in 1959.

The fishing fleet is much reduced, but Ucluelet's Boat Basin is still a busy place.

The *Maquinna*

It makes sense that one of the most fondly remembered personalities from the days before the Port Alberni road arrived was not a person but a ship, the SS *Princess Maquinna*. Built and based in Victoria by the Canadian Pacific Railway, the *Maquinna* was the West Coast's lifeline to civilization for more than 40 years. Every 10 days she slipped the Belleville Street dock and set out on a six-day circuit, stopping at Port Renfrew, Bamfield, Ucluelet, Tofino, Tahsis, Zeballos and Port Alice plus a host of canneries, camps and waypoints in between. At settlements too small to have a dock, she would heave to and unload freight, passengers and sometimes livestock into bobbing work boats. Much of the affection evoked by the tubby coaster was directed to the person of her master, Captain Edward Gillam, who skippered her for 20 years. Gillam willingly performed mercy runs, abandoning his schedule to rescue an injured person or a mother in labour, and not a few West Coasters could boast the good ship *Maquinna* as their place of birth. The whole coast went into mourning when Captain Gillam died in a fall aboard ship, and when the doughty *Maquinna* was finally decommissioned in 1952, it marked the end of an era.

Top: Old-time cottages add character to the Ucluelet waterfront.

Above: Manager Gale Johnsen welcomes the world to Ucluelet's Du Quah Native arts gallery.

Right: Seafood fresh off the boat is one of the attractions of the Ucluelet waterfront.

In the 1960s, the Brynnor Iron Mine came into production just outside of Ucluelet, employing between 150 and 200 people. Although it stopped producing in 1966, its brief existence was an incentive to improve and pave the road to Port Alberni. The flooded pit is now a favoured swimming spot out on the road toward Toquart Bay. Logging continued as the town's mainstay throughout the 1970s and '80s. The progress of the forest industry can be read in the shape of the hills above town, which are barbered up to the skyline like most of the hills along Highway 4, and indeed throughout Vancouver Island. As loggers cut the good timber in the valleys and worked their way through the smaller trees on the upper slopes, their attention turned northward to the last few untouched watersheds around Clayoquot Sound, setting the stage for a historic confrontation with those who believed that this last glorious remnant of the temperate rain forest should be saved in its natural state.

Ucluelet seemed always to have some sort of industry booming. Tofino, always poor and out of luck, became known as Tough City. But by the 1990s, the positions began slowly to reverse. Tofino cast its lot with the emerging tourism and recreation economy, providing services to a growing flood of Pacific Rim Park patrons, while Ucluelet elected to stand pat with the logging and fishing industries traditional to the area. Tofino became the base for environmental activism aimed at preserving Clayoquot's old-growth forest, and the historic rivalry between the two rim towns heightened. Media played up the contrast in styles, ascribing a new-age, flower-child persona to Tofino and a no-nonsense "working Joe" persona to Ucluelet. Although this was an oversimplification, since loggers and supporters of logging lived in both communities, and the clash of values pitted neighbour against neighbour, the comparison had some basis in reality: Ucluelet loggers blamed Tofino "tree huggers" for shutting down the woods and putting them out of work.

Ucluelet's Amphitrite Point Lighthouse guards the northern entrance to Barkley Sound.

The Protest of '93

The eyes of the world were on Clayoquot in the summer of 1993 as 12,000 people came to the "Black Hole" protest camp in a burned-over logging slash near Ucluelet. Most protestors were Canadian, but others came from the USA, Europe and Australia. It was the climax of a decade of skirmishes aimed at saving the Clayoquot rain forest and their aim was to stop loggers from going to work across the Kennedy River bridge. By the time the dust cleared, 932 protestors had been arrested, making it the largest act of civil disobedience in Canadian history. Most protestors were normally law-abiding citizens and not all of them were young. A number of them received jail terms of up to six months, and fines as high as $3,000. One was a 66-year-old grandmother named Betty Krawczyk. At her sentencing in the fall of 1993, she told the judge, "I promised those poor bleeding mountains behind my house at Cypress Bay, that are still bleeding from those landslides from the clearcuts of 10 years ago, that I would come home with my shield or on it, and I intend to do that, sir." As a result of the environmental campaign, MacMillan Bloedel, the area's major forest company, eventually laid off all 77 workers in its Kennedy Lake Camp, and the volume of timber cut in the Clayoquot region dropped from a high of 959,000 cubic metres in 1988 to a low of 24,000 cubic metres in 2000.

To make the economic adjustment harder for Ucluelet, commercial fishing collapsed in the 1990s, halving the number of jobs. At the same time, Tofino's tourism economy boomed, in no small part because of publicity generated by the logging protest. Between 1982 and 2002, Tofino's population more than doubled, from 715 to 1,549, while Ucluelet's population remained static, growing only from 1,624 to 1,646. In 2001 the average price of a home in Tofino was almost double that in Ucluelet.

Having watched Tofino surge forward on the tourism wave, Ucluelet belatedly got into the act. In recent years, new resorts, galleries and coffee shops have breathed fresh life into the town. "Ucluelet is the hot spot right now for business start-up. And it's all tourism," says a local banker. Ucluelet was reporting an average of 10 new business incorporations annually through the late 1990s, compared with only three in Tofino.

Anti-logging protestors being arrested during the 1992 blockade at Clayoquot Arm.
Mark Hobson

Two competitors give it their all in the ladies' two-man saw buck at Ukee Days.

Ucluelet pioneer George Fraser gained world renown for his breeding of rhododendrons and roses.

The West Coast was explored and settled by water, and the best way to see Barkley Sound is by boat. The MV *Lady Rose* still delivers mail and freight in the Sound, departing from Port Alberni several times weekly year-round, with scheduled stops to Kildonan (Uchucklesaht) and Bamfield. In the summer there are more sailings, and the *Lady Rose* and her sister ship, the MV *Frances Barkley*, provide daily service throughout the Sound, with added stops at the Broken Group Islands and Ucluelet. To sail through Barkley Sound on these historic ships is to recapture times of the past, when roads were just wishful thinking and boats were the only means of transport.

Ucluelet is a stepping stone to Barkley Sound. Whale-watching tours start in March, with the annual migration of thousands of gray whales northward just offshore. Whalefest, an annual event celebrated by both Ucluelet and Tofino, marks the arrival of the migrating gray whales with boat tours. Viewing points on land in Ucluelet and the adjacent Pacific Rim National Park Reserve are staffed by telescope-toting naturalists and park rangers.

Ucluelet's First Flower Child

Ucluelet was a small, obscure place at the end of the 19th century, but on the map of world rhododendron breeders, it loomed larger than New York, thanks to the presence of George Fraser, an English horticulturist. Fraser had once risen to the position of head gardener of a British estate but chose to emigrate to the Canadian west coast, where he could create his own estate among the salmonberries and cedar trees. On a 95-hectare pre-emption now occupied by half of downtown Ucluelet, he developed a landmark garden and nursery, supplying the Canadian Pacific Railway with plants for its showplace gardens, and shipping orders to city customers in crates made of driftwood. In his spare time he pursued a passion for crossbreeding and hybridizing rhododendrons, keeping up a busy correspondence with experts around the world. In 1920 he achieved immortality by being the first person successfully to hybridize *Rhododendron canadense*, the native rhododendron of eastern North America, producing the variant ever after known to gardeners of the world as *Rhododendron fraseri*. He also created a popular rose by crossing the native Nootka rose with the hybrid tea Richmond. Fraser found time to be a good citizen of Ucluelet, donating 4.5 hectares to the Athletic Club and school, and playing his violin at local dances well into his 80s. He died in 1944, at age 90. In 1990, when the American Rhododendron Society posthumously awarded him the Pioneer's Achievement Award, he became only the fourth person to be so honoured. The George Fraser Memorial Garden, beside the school in Ucluelet, has many specimen rhodos as well as a plaque bearing the names of Ucluelet's first settlers.

Whale-watching continues through the summer months as some whales stay to feed in fertile nearshore waters. Sea kayakers take advantage of this period of stable weather and calm seas to explore the waters of Barkley Sound. The Broken Group, a sprinkling of small forested islets within Pacific Rim Park, is a prime destination for kayakers planning long-distance adventures. For paddlers with open ocean experience, it can be reached by a long sea-crossing from either Ucluelet or Toquart Bay. For those who do not want to brave the open water, the *Lady Rose* and *Frances Barkley* transport paddlers as well as their kayaks straight to the Broken Group from either Port Alberni or Ucluelet during the summer months. And beginner paddlers can sign up for day trips around Ucluelet, or overnight trips to the Broken Group, led by experienced guides.

As Ucluelet's economy turns around, the nature of the community itself is changing. In the town that survived by razing the rain forest for so long, there is a growing awareness that preserving the area's natural beauty will create more jobs in the long run. The new Wild Pacific Trail, a winding course over the rocky headlands at the tip of the Ucluth Peninsula, is symbolic of Ucluelet's path to the new economy. The tourism boom brings hope to this boom-and-bust town: that it has finally found an industry that will endure.

A coastal black-tailed deer on the beach of Clarke Island in the Broken Group.

4 Long Beach

A S LONG AS A CENTURY AGO, THE EXPANSIVE WAVE-WASHED SANDS OF LONG BEACH WERE ALREADY A TOURIST DRAW. ACCESS WAS DIFFICULT, BUT EVEN IN THE EARLY 1900S, VISITORS FROM THE UNITED STATES WERE STEPPING ASHORE IN TOFINO AND UCLUELET FROM THE *PRINCESS MAQUINNA* TO SEE THE FAMED BEACHES FIRST-HAND.

The graceful sweep of Long Beach forms the centrepiece of Pacific Rim National Park Reserve.

Long Beach was also a cherished destination for the settlers in the area, a chance to get away from it all for a weekend of picnicking, bathing in the sea and gathering around the campfire.

Today, Long Beach is still the Pacific Rim's most impressive and renowned geographical feature, and the ultimate destination of many travellers to the West Coast. The shoreline between Tofino and Ucluelet consists mainly of a series of broad sandy beaches, punctuated by rocky headlands that are pounded by endless surf. The chain of beaches stretches from wave-washed Half Moon Bay and Florencia Bay, northwest to Wickaninnish Bay, Combers Beach, Long Beach proper and on to Schooner Cove and the sandy beaches below Radar Hill—a distance of over 20 kilometres. The beaches have been formed by the interplay between changing sea levels, the action of waves and currents, the creation and movement of sand, and the chance shaping of the coastal geography by glaciers.

Sea levels rose and fell dramatically in the millennia following the end of the last ice age. At times, the area that is now Long Beach was flooded, and waves lapped at hill slopes that are now far inland. At other times the shoreline lay many kilometres out to sea from where the beach is now. By 7,000 years ago, sea levels had stabilized to within a few metres of present levels. The coast had finally started to bear some resemblance to its present-day form.

Sand appears on the coast in many ways: pushed in from the deeper ocean by wave action, tumbled down rivers, or carried along the coast by longshore currents that send the grains rolling and skipping along the sea floor. At Long Beach, much of the sand has formed from the mounds of glacial till left on the coast by glaciers. Thousands of years of wave action have crushed and sorted the grains. Softer minerals have been ground away to flecks of clay and then swept away by the currents, leaving clean, round grains of quartz sand behind.

Beach sand is not something that usually captures our attention, but it deserves a closer look. At first it may all seem the same, but if you scoop up a bit and examine it with a magnifying glass, the diversity of the tiny grains may surprise you. Sand from the dunes at the back of the beaches is very fine and well sorted. It consists mostly of quartz grains, all rounded to about a fifth of a millimetre in size, and shaped and winnowed by the wind. Lower down, on the tidal part of the beach, wave action sorts the sand, both by grain size and by composition, into colourful stripes. The white stripes are formed of the lightest grains, mostly crushed shells: a close look will often reveal fragments of white clam shell, purple mussel shell and the occasional pink sea urchin spine, and sometimes flat, shiny grains of mica as well. The dark stripes are formed of heavy minerals such as magnetite and garnet. A century ago miners were even extracting gold dust from these heavy layers down at Florencia Bay! The bulk of the sand is a complete blend: crushed shells mixed with grains of rock and mineral, mostly quartz, all sorted and rounded by the incessant movement of the waves.

At Long Beach, the accumulation of sand is far more extensive than we can see. It continues far inland under the rain forest, in deposits left thousands of years ago when sea levels were higher. The sand also forms the ocean floor for many kilometres out to sea.

Except for the occasional seabird, the shifting sands of Long Beach at first seem devoid of life. The beach, like every other environment on the coast, is actually an

Sunset viewed through the rocks at the north end of Long Beach.

Top: The shell of a razor clam attests to unseen marine life swarming below the surface of beach sands.

Above: A giant green anemone opens like an exotic flower in a rocky tide pool.

extremely specialized ecosystem with a diversity of inhabitants, each occupying a very specific niche. Only here, much of the action happens out of sight, below the surface of the sand.

The beach is a zone of constant movement. Even on the calmest of days, waves lap at the shore and stir up sand in the shallows, and the shoreline shifts constantly with the rise and fall of the tide. The beach can be divided into three zones: the dunes, their edge marked by a line of driftwood tossed by winter storm swells; the backshore between the dunes and the average high-tide mark; and the foreshore, or intertidal zone, that zone that wets and dries twice daily with the rise and fall of the tide.

Beneath the wet sands of the intertidal zone live many and diverse strange creatures. Tiny organisms called plankton—microscopic plants and animals—that live between the sand grains are the key to this community, the food source for clams, worms and buried sea anemones.

Razor clams, whose elongated shells shine pink and white like porcelain, are common on Long Beach. A razor clam sits vertically in the sand with only its siphon sticking up above the surface, filtering plankton from the seawater. When threatened, it uses its muscular foot to burrow downward with amazing speed. Two hundred species of clams live along the coast, with specialized shell shapes and feeding habits that depend upon the characteristics of the shoreline they inhabit: an active, wave-washed beach with clean sand, or tranquil tidal mud flats carpeted with algae and other seaweeds. Many of these clams make good eating and are harvested over the winter months both for local chowder bowls as well as for the commercial market.

Another resident under the sands is the clamworm. This is a large worm, up to 30 centimetres in length, brown or purplish in colour, with numerous feathery legs down each side of its body. For most of the year these worms live out of sight, burrowing through the gravel and sand, but in early summer they emerge from the depths in a mating frenzy. Rising to the surface of the sea, often on the night of a full moon, they swim wildly about as the females disperse eggs through the water and the males spread their sperm.

Crabs, sea stars and sand dollars make their home in the shallow waters just beyond the low-tide mark. Sand dollars, which are related to sea urchins, cruise the shallow sea floor below the waves, devouring scraps of seaweed and other detritus. The sand dollar is covered in tiny hair-like spines with which it can steer food toward its mouth opening on the bottom of its shell. Storm waves may toss entire colonies of sand dollars onto the beach, where they soon perish, their bleached shells a prized trophy of beachwalkers.

Many predators patrol the intertidal zone. When the tide is high, fish such as sand sole and staghorn sculpin glide over the sandy bottom, gobbling up clams, worms and small fish. Tiny crustaceans that look like miniature shrimp, called isopods, live in the sand. They chew on any dead matter they come across, occasionally giving a sharp bite to the bare ankle of a beachwalker. Their close relatives, the amphipods, hop around higher up on the beach, earning their nickname "sand fleas" as they scavenge for food around piles of washed-up kelp. At low tide, avian predators swoop

down to the sand—crows digging for clams, and eagles on the lookout for practically anything that washes up.

Many types of sandpipers also feed at the beach. Some, like sanderlings, least sandpipers and western sandpipers, probe the beach with touch-sensitive beaks in search of worms, their tiny legs a blur as they move up and down the beach in time with each wave. Others, like the semipalmated plover, feed alone, standing motionless higher up the beach. When their sharp eyes spy a movement, they scurry across the sand to pull up the unlucky worm. Shorebirds can be seen on the beach at any time of the year, but are especially abundant in early May, during the spring migration, and in the winter.

Beaches are separated by jagged rocky headlands. With a tidal range of up to 4 metres, the surf that almost reaches the trees may, only a few hours later, be lapping at the rocks far below, leaving tranquil pools in the uneven outcrops. These tide pools are home to colourful plants and animals that are incredible in their toughness to withstand the most diverse of conditions. At high tide, the pools are flooded with salt water and pounded by forceful waves. At low tide, the pools and rock slopes may be subject to fresh-water rains, and conditions ranging from the drying heat of the midsummer sun to winter frost and snow. Anemones, starfish, barnacles, mussels and crabs cling to the rocks, either attached to the rock face itself or wedged in cracks, miraculously adapted to this most extreme environment.

Purple sea stars cluster in a crevice to escape the pounding surf.

You never know what treasures you may find on a stroll along the beach.

California sea lions
congregate on Sea Lion
Rocks off Long Beach.

Long Beach today retains little evidence of its long history of human inhabitants. Its southern stretches lie within the territory of the Ucluelet nation, and the northern part belongs to the Tla-o-qui-aht. The Tla-o-qui-aht village of Esowista is home to about 150 residents.

Clubbed to Death

Many hundreds of years ago, long before white men arrived on the West Coast, the ancestors of the Tla-o-qui-aht lived around Kennedy Lake. A different tribe occupied Long Beach. Tla-o-qui-aht were famed warriors, feared by other tribes. Desiring to expand their territory out to the ocean, they descended upon the village at Long Beach, killed the people there and claimed the village as their own territory. The name of the village today, Esowista (pronounced "Hiss-OW-is-ta"), means "clubbed to death."

In the early 1900s, Long Beach was home to several homesteaders. It was also an important land connection between Tofino and Ucluelet, bypassing the nearly impenetrable rain forest. The usual route was by boat with the rising tide from Tofino to the top of Grice Bay, then crossing the peninsula via a short trail out to Long Beach. Travellers would then walk the length of Long Beach, all the way to the end of Florencia Bay (then known as Wreck Bay), and cross the top of the Ucluth Peninsula along the Willowbrae Road to the end of Ucluelet Inlet, where they were picked up by boat to travel the last part of the journey to Ucluelet. Travellers who could not

Above: Kenny David of Esowista shows off the cedar bark hat woven for him by his grandmother.

Left: Compact Esowista Village is surrounded by the Pacific Rim National Park Reserve.

arrange boat pickups had to walk the entire distance, following rough paths through the rain forest between Tofino and Long Beach and then between Long Beach and Ucluelet. The journey usually took two full days, including a stop for the night with homesteaders on Long Beach.

One of these homesteaders was G.A.B. Jackson, who lived during the late 1920s on central Long Beach, where the main parking lots are now. His diary, with brief but daily entries from 1927 to 1929, records the steady flow of travellers who passed his homestead and provides insight into what day-to-day life really was like for the settlers. Jackson had a couple of horses and a herd of cows, and was also visited by wild cows. He worked as a telegraph lineman, maintaining the central part of the line between Ucluelet and Tofino. He lived on the products of his farm—vegetables, chickens, eggs, cows—and on what he could collect from the wild by digging clams, picking berries and shooting ducks and deer. He became friends with the Natives from nearby Esowista, whom he called the "Siwashes," and he learned to speak their language. Jackson's diary for 1927 includes these entries:

February 19:

Still blowing this morning and continued squally all day with rain. Line down east from Ucluelet—mine all ok. Shot eight wigeon with three shells this morning. Surf tossed logs on beach at high tide. Sea very rough. Opened fresh sack wheat for chickens today. Johnnie Johnson dead in Victoria. Hens all laying good.

February 20:

Gale continues all day, S.S.W. Thunder and lightning, rain, hail, wind. Sea very rough. Line ok at Toquart.

February 21:

Storm abating W. wind and some rain. Frost came in from Tofino on the tide this afternoon will stay the night with us. Joe Hays and another Indian brought in the skiff that I lost last Nov. all intact—boots, oars and oarlocks—charged me six dollars for finding it and returning it to me.

February 22:

Weather fine again. Frost walked through to Ucluelet and took our mail out, went as far as the Point with him—cut wood in afternoon. Rained in evening and at night.

Cadborosaurus

Vancouver Island has its very own sea monster. Although no carcasses of the creature have ever made their way into any laboratories, enough scientists agree that it may exist that it has earned a Latin name: *Cadborosaurus williamsii*, after Cadboro Bay in Victoria, where most of the sitings have taken place. It is thought to be a relative of other legendary sea serpents, such as the Loch Ness monster and Lake Okanagan's infamous resident Ogopogo.

The sea serpent has been a part of First Nations traditions for millennia. It first came to the attention of the coast's white inhabitants with a spate of sightings in the 1930s. There are about 300 sightings of Cadborosaurus on record, and an average of half a dozen new sightings every year. Very consistent descriptions tell of a serpent-like creature up 20 metres long, with a long, snake-like neck and a small head, often travelling rapidly through the water with its neck curled into one or two small humps behind the head.

Present-day visitors to the coast may respond to stories of Cadborosaurus with disbelief, but Jackson's 1927 matter-of-fact diary entries show that in his time, the creature's existence was in no doubt.

July 27:

Fine and warm. Norma and I took a walk this evening as far as Cannon ravine saw six deer only out fifty minutes. They are quite plentiful lately. Two other fishermen besides the Indians say they saw the big sea serpent off Long Beach last week.

July 28:

Thick fog all day today no sea and calm. Susie and I dug a bucket of razor clams this a.m.— worked in garden. Took a walk in evening and did not see any deer. The fishermen report seeing the big sea serpent off Nootka—several of them saw it and gave chase for three miles shot at it several times but did not get it. They all agree in their reports that it is about 75 feet long and the general description is much the same. A C.P.C. seine crew also saw it off Esperanza Inlet. They tried for three hours to get it in a seine net but did not get him—they say it was in plain sight for most of three hours.

No further entries mention the enigmatic creature.

Opposite: Storm-tossed driftwood clusters near the mouth of Sandhill Creek at Combers Beach.

Following pages: The dying light of a winter sunset illuminates storm surf at South Beach, just south of Wickaninnish Bay.

In 1923 a rough road from Ucluelet to Long Beach was completed, and a government truck was the first vehicle to drive the beach. (Cars and trucks were brought to the area by boat, from Port Alberni or Victoria, to Ucluelet.) By late 1927, a road connected northern Long Beach to Tofino. The roads were passable to horses, but they were not so reliable for wheeled transport. Cars and trucks frequently bogged in gullies on the rough tracks, and vehicles had to be driven along the beach at low tide and with an insider's knowledge of where the soft spots were. Vehicles that got stuck in the sand were swallowed by the rising tide. Through the 1930s, construction proceeded on a road that bypassed Long Beach, mainly as a make-work project during the Depression. By the beginning of World War II, a new road connected Ucluelet and Tofino.

During the war years, numerous fears were engendered by the fact that Canada's west coast was "undefended," and therefore a possible first target for any attack by Japan. Protective measures were taken: nighttime blackouts were enforced, and pilings were driven into Long Beach and Chesterman Beach to prevent any landing by Japanese craft.

The giant runways of the otherwise small Tofino airport, and the military installations at Radar Hill, are all relics of the fearful days of the 1940s and early '50s. By 1957, these radar installations and the Tofino airport were closed. The airport's long runways are still maintained, however. Today they are used by small commuter airlines from Vancouver and Seattle, and they are an emergency landing site for commercial aircraft travelling between North America and Asia.

Neil and Marilyn Buckle lived on Long Beach from the late 1950s until it was gazetted as a national park in the early 1970s. Long-time residents of the coast, they have a wealth of stories to tell about its past.

Neil's father bought 20 hectares at Combers Beach in 1951, "all the land that is washing away now," says Neil, and he and Marilyn started up the Combers Beach Resort there. They recall the opening of the new road, which finally connected the coast to Port Alberni.

The road was completed in 1959, a winding gravel logging road full of tight switchbacks creeping up steep hillsides. A locked gate at Sproat Lake prevented general access except during evenings and nights. In August 1959, 74 vehicles from Tofino and Ucluelet, accompanied by logging trucks, made the inaugural trip over Sutton Pass to the town of Port Alberni. Neil drove his '54 Ford pickup across as part of that first "cavalcade." He chuckles as he recalls the day: "There was a spot where, for low-slung cars, they had to pull them through with a bulldozer. We just rammed on through. As soon as we got to pavement, we all started racing one another. We went all the way to Victoria!"

Marilyn rolls her eyes. "Everyone I'm sure was imbibing," she says.

The new road provided greater access to the area, and along with waves of tourists came the first hippies. Marilyn remembers hippies and beatniks starting to arrive in 1963 and '64. "They started coming and my God did they come! Wreck Bay was wall-to-wall plastic shelters. As soon as we got to the Long Beach road in our truck, all these guys with long hair would be hitchhiking, so we'd say 'Into the back!' and off we'd go to Ukie. We'd go to the church bazaar, where you could get all you could eat for 25 cents, and they would go there and fill their baggies."

A bleached sand dollar shell.

The long, rolling breakers of Long Beach also attracted the area's first surfers. Back then, Canada's surfing scene was nearly non-existent, and only a few hard-core surfers travelled to the remote shores to brave the icy waters. Today Long Beach is renowned for its surf. In summer the gently peeling waves are perfect for beginners on surfboards and boogie boards, although all swimmers must beware of the strong currents. On a big day in winter, however, only the strongest and most experienced world-class surfers, clad from head to toe in five-millimetre neoprene, dare to attempt to paddle through the frothing white water to the break.

By the early 1970s, Long Beach had long been regarded by its many visitors as a national treasure, and for decades there had been rumblings about preserving it as a national park. On May 4, 1971, the talk became reality: Pacific Rim National Park Reserve was dedicated at Long Beach, in the presence of Princess Anne and then Minister of Northern Affairs Jean Chrétien. Landowners such as Neil and Marilyn Buckle were forced to sell their properties, and the hippies and squatters were evicted.

Beachcombing

The open ocean beaches of the West Coast make it a paradise for beachcombers. Treasures range from shells to bamboo poles to Nike running shoes. For years the most sought-after prizes have been the tinted glass balls that occupy places of honour on mantels throughout the region. Ranging in diameter from 10 to 45 centimetres and in colour from clear to amber to black, the crudely made globes originate in Asia, where they are still used to buoy up fish nets, though plastic is taking over. Some make the crossing in six months, while others cycle for decades in a system of currents called the North Pacific Gyre and arrive on the coast festooned with growth. And the Nikes? Well, on May 27, 1990, the container ship *Hansa Carrier* lost a deckload of 80,000 Nike shoes in a mid-ocean storm and they have been washing ashore around the Pacific Rim ever since. In 1992 another ship lost 29,000 bathtub toys, and plastic beavers, turtles and ducks began turning up in beach flotsam. The duckies gained cult status when oceanographers began using them to track ocean currents, and the manufacturer, First Years Inc., posted a $100-per-duck bounty. Cute as they are, the toys are symptomatic of an ugly problem. Freighters lose 10,000 shipping containers overboard every year, and their spilled contents are just one contributor to a continent of garbage building in the North Pacific Gyre, like "a toilet that never flushes," to quote the Washington oceanographer Curtis Ebermeyer. West Coast beachcombers do not wander far before encountering fallout from this mass, and they'll be lucky if it is anything as charming as a duckie.

Pacific Rim is dedicated as a National Park "Reserve" because First Nations claims to the land have not yet been settled. The Tla-o-qui-aht are the original owners of northern Long Beach as well as of the surrounding regions to the north and east. For now, the Canadian government has allocated them a small reserve at the north end of Long Beach, their ancestral village of Esowista.

Today, the Long Beach unit of Pacific Rim National Park Reserve receives about one million visitors a year. Many are accommodated in Tofino or Ucluelet, but Greenpoint campground, on Long Beach itself, has 94 tent and trailer sites—most of which are reserved many months in advance. Recreational use of the park is mainly for day use: surfing, hiking or simply hanging out on the beach. Numerous short hiking trails are signposted with natural history interpretation. Many have boardwalks, not only for ease of access but also to protect delicate ecosystems.

For hikers looking for a longer trek, there is the Nuu-chah-nulth Trail from Wickaninnish Beach to Florencia Bay: traversing this beach you can hike back up to the highway along the old Willowbrae Road. Or you can follow in the footsteps of the old-timers, hiking along any of the park trails that lead down to Long Beach, then along the beach for as many miles as you want, returning to the highway by a different trail.

Grice Bay is a shallow bay that lies within Pacific Rim park, on the sheltered northeast side of the Esowista Peninsula. The bay is tidal. At high tide, fronds of eelgrass rise through the shallow water and touch its surface. At low tide the water empties out, leaving sticky mud flats pocked with little holes that mark the burrows of ghost shrimp. In some years, gray whales spend the entire summer feeding in the

Contestants await their turn in a surfing competition. Pacific Rim beaches bring world-class challengers to vie with local talent.

Wolf sightings are increasing even at the more popular beaches.

shallows of Grice Bay on ghost shrimp and tiny clams, swimming out to adjacent deep-water channels twice a day as the bay empties. More than half of the bay is ghost shrimp habitat, but only small, young whales can access the shallows. Parts of the bay are too shallow to admit any whales at all, a natural control that prevents the whales from ever over-harvesting this important food source.

In all, Pacific Rim National Park Reserve covers a stretch of 125 kilometres of Vancouver Island's wild outer coast, from Long Beach to the Broken Group Islands and down to the West Coast Trail, which heads south from Barkley Sound. The Long Beach unit consists of 13,715 hectares, of which just over half are on land and the remainder are on the ocean. This area is habitat for wolves, bears, deer and gray whales—all of which are seen frequently—as well as countless smaller animals and plants. It is a relatively untouched fragment of coastal temperate rain forest and the adjacent nearshore marine environment. However, it is one of the most threatened national parks in the country.

The park is ultimately a very narrow strip of shoreline. Industrial logging still takes place right up to the park boundaries. The Tofino airport, which lies within the park, suffers from heavy contamination of chemicals spilled or dumped during the less enlightened times of the 1940s and '50s. The salmon streams whose outlets to the ocean lie within protected parkland still, for the most part, flow through industrial areas and through this contamination.

Wild animals do not recognize park boundaries: bears that live within the park also amble across the highway to Tofino's garbage dump, where they may be shot. The high number of visitors to the park invariably has an impact on the environment and on wildlife, no matter how sensitive and well intentioned those visitors may be. Bears and wolves become habituated to campers' food or garbage, and they frequent inhabited areas, where they can end up being hit by cars, or being shot because as habituated animals they are considered to be a danger. Visitors' dogs attract wolves and actually may promote wolf attacks and wolf-human interactions. Even people strolling quietly on the beach have an impact on the ecosystem. For thousands of years the beaches have been a crucial feeding stop for shorebirds such as sandpipers migrating between areas near Mexico and the Arctic. Every time a flock takes to the wing as someone walks past, the birds are burning valuable calories instead of fattening up for the next leg of their journey.

Long Beach is indeed a national treasure. It is the wild edge itself: the meeting of serene rain forest and turbulent ocean, a place of both spectacular beauty and great environmental significance. Home to the Nuu-chah-nulth for millennia, it is now also a place close to the heart of millions of travellers. And although it is wild and rugged, at the same time it is fragile. With good planning and some good luck, this treasure will always be treated as such, and it and all of its inhabitants will be here for the generations to come.

Wreck of the *Carelmapu*

One of the coast's tragic shipwrecks occurred off Long Beach on November 23, 1915, when the Chilean windjammer *Carelmapu* was caught in a seasonal gale. The storm drove the helpless vessel along the island shore toward Gowlland Rocks at the western end of Long Beach. Captain Desholmes dropped his anchors, but they didn't take hold until the ship was a few cables off the foaming reef.

The coastal steamer *Princess Maquinna* was at this time making her southward run from Tofino, but the weather was so wild that Captain Gillam was about to turn back. Just then he spotted the wallowing form of the *Carelmapu* near shore, flying distress flags. At great risk to his own vessel and its full list of passengers, Gillam manoeuvred as close to the stricken vessel as he dared, but the raging seas made it impossible to affix a towline. When the *Carelmapu* tried to send over a lifeboat, the boat overturned in the surf, drowning all seven occupants. Reluctantly, Gillam gave up the rescue and proceeded to Ucluelet, where he contacted the Tofino lifeboat, but it was unable to reach the scene until the following morning. By that time the *Carelmapu* had been driven onto the reef and broken up, drowning all but six of her 24 hands. For years the ship's bones were still visible at low tide, and according to Anthony Guppy, a local author, there is a legend that if you stand on the beach in the late fall when the cold, damp wind is urging the fog along in ghostly patches, you can hear faint cries of lost sailors mingling with the roar of the surf.

5
The Tofino Area

THE VILLAGE OF TOFINO
RESTS UPON A ROCKY
KNOB THAT IS ALMOST AN
ISLAND, CONNECTED TO THE
REST OF VANCOUVER ISLAND BY
A NARROW FORESTED TONGUE
OF LAND: THE ESOWISTA
PENINSULA.

Tofino's First Street dock is the focal point
of Clayoquot Sound boating activity.

Thousands of years ago, when sea levels were raised by melting ice after the ice age, this knob actually *was* an island, and what is now the peninsula was a wave-washed sandspit, just like the spit that connects Frank Island to Chesterman Beach today. With falling sea levels, a forest grew on the spit, and it is easy to forget from the tree-fringed highway here that ocean lies within a few hundred metres on *both* sides of you.

Today, geologists can figure out the local earth history by reading the signs in deposits left by the glaciers and by wave action. Walking along any of the trails or roads that cross the peninsula behind Chesterman Beach, you can see the sandy banks left by former shorelines as the sea dropped. The Nuu-chah-nulth people were here not long after the ice retreated, and some of their place names and traditions may reflect geological changes that they saw over centuries.

The village of Opitsat, visible straight across the harbour from the docks at Tofino, has been a principal village for millennia. From here, they voyaged out on hunting and fishing trips, occupying different beaches and river mouths as seasonal camps for gathering food. The rocky headland at Tofino's northern shore is Naachaks ("lookout"), a good place to keep watch for any canoes approaching the important village of Opitsat. The local word for the area around south Chesterman Beach is Tahsis, the "passage where you can go through." It is narrow enough to walk across even today, but in the far past it would have been narrow enough that people could drag canoes across it from the protected harbour to the open ocean, saving the long trip around Naachaks. The small island at the entrance to the harbour is called Echachist, which means "rising up," a strange name for such a low island, unless it

The village of Tofino spreads across the tip of Esowista Peninsula, with Wickaninnish, Felice, Stubbs and Vargas islands in the background.

refers to it having emerged like a reef at low tide as global sea levels fell. Many Nuu-chah-nulth groups have stories of floods, some of which may refer to rapid rises in sea level after the ice age, which in the space of a few generations would have forced them to relocate their seafront villages.

After the massacre of the *Tonquin*'s crew in 1811, white traders avoided Clayoquot Sound for many years. By the 1850s, nearly two generations had passed since the *Tonquin* incident, and a new traffic in fur seal pelts brought white men back to the area. In 1855 a trading post was established on Stubbs Island, a small island with a lovely crescent beach a stone's throw across Duffin Pass from present-day Tofino. When Frederick Thornberg took charge of Clayoquot Station in 1874, relations with the Tla-o-qui-aht were still not easy. "I traded through a hole in the end of the building," Thornberg wrote; "it was about two feet wide and two Indians could just stand and look in with their elbows and breasts leaning on the bottom part of the hole." At first Thornberg had difficulty communicating, as "few of the Indians understood the Hudsons Bay Company giberets called Chenook, but I soon learnet to talk the Indian Dialect. I had great help from middle aget Indian named Gwiar." Gwiar was an outcast because he had been the father of twins—grounds for ostracism in Nuu-chah-nulth society—and he was a great friend to Thornberg, but unfortunately he fell ill. "I went over to his shack and he lay in bed and looket very bad. I askt him if I could doe any thing for him. He replayet no, the medicine you have will doe me no good. I seen a Jhe-haa. That means an Indian Devil and if anyone sees him it is a very bad sign. In three days he was Death. Indians of the West Coast were very superstitious." Thornberg left Clayoquot Station to take over a post at

Tofino rhodo gardener Ken Gibson says of his 2,500 plants, "It takes me the whole day to get around and say 'hi' to each one."

Tofino started out as a trading post called Clayoquot on lovely Stubbs Island, a stone's throw from the present townsite.

Ahousat in 1885, but one of his sons, Freddy, was still living on Stubbs Island in the 1960s.

Throughout the late 1800s, outsiders flooded in to Clayoquot Sound—traders on sealing ships, Chinese miners working remote rivers for gold, fishermen and fish processors to salt and export the salmon and missionaries to save lost souls. The trading post on Stubbs Island spawned a small commercial centre comprising a store, a school, a post office, a jail and a hotel, which was granted BC's Liquor Licence Number 1. This village came to be known simply as Clayoquot.

From the 1880s to the early part of the next century, many settlers arrived in Clayoquot Sound, pre-empting land in an attempt to carve a life out of the wild rain forest. Some came from England and Scotland, others from Norway and the United States. The descendants of many of these original families live in Tofino today, and the family names live on in and around town: Grice Point, Arnet Island, Eik Landing. By 1899, the population of Clayoquot was listed as 150 whites and 250 Natives. Few of them resided in the settlement of Clayoquot itself. Most were working on distant islands and up remote inlets, developing mining prospects, operating sawmills, working in canneries and trying their luck as farmers.

Tofino's St. Columba Church, built in 1913, still stands at the corner of 2nd and Main.

Tofino's waterfront profile is backdropped by the forested slopes of Meares Island's Mt. Colnett.

St. Columba Church

St. Columba Church was built in 1913. Half of the funds for the church were donated by the family of a deceased man in England for a church to be built in his memory "on the most beautiful spot on Vancouver Island." The rest of the money was raised by local parishioners. This church still stands in Tofino, at the corner of 2nd and Main.

The population of Clayoquot grew slowly, and finally residents recognized that they needed more land than tiny Stubbs Island could provide. In 1912 the townsite

of present-day Tofino was purchased from homesteader John Grice, and the streets were surveyed. The name *Tofino* was borrowed from nearby Tofino Inlet, which in turn was named after the early Spanish navigator Vincente Tofiño de San Miguel. By 1932, when Tofino was incorporated as a village, it consisted of Main Street (just a muddy track with a two-plank sidewalk), a few short cross streets and a handful of buildings scattered along the water's edge. First Street led down to the government wharf, still the marine transportation centre for the region today. Tofino resident Islay McLeod was a child in those days, and today she rejoices at the view of the mountains from Campbell Street. "In those days we couldn't see the mountains or the glaciers from town. Main Street is too low, down by the water, and up here on Campbell Street, well, it was all thick forest here back then!"

South of Tofino, other homesteaders were trying their luck on the land. The area now known as Chesterman Beach was pre-empted in May 1900 by John Chesterman, whose homestead was located just across the highway from present-day Chesterman Beach Road, on the inlet side. Chesterman was an important Tofino personage in the early part of the century. He, along with the Arnet family, pushed for a school in the area, but the two families did not have enough children between them to qualify for provincial assistance. Chesterman managed to persuade the Lennard Island lighthouse-keeper, Francis Garrard, to participate, even though the Garrard children had to row a canoe in from the island on Mondays and row back out

Above: Commercial sea-urchin fishermen offload their catch on Tofino's First Street dock.

Left: "It doesn't have to be pretty to be tasty!" Fisherman shows off the gaping maw of a codfish at Fourth Street dock.

Top: The entrance to
Tofino's fascinating
Botanical Gardens.

Above: Historian and
former prospector, Walter
Guppy is author of several
books about Tofino.

to the lighthouse on Fridays, and the school was granted. Chesterman also served as coxswain on Tofino's lifeboat, which at that time was powered only by oars. He staked a mining claim on Meares Island, and in 1913 his Calapa Mine produced 1,350 tonnes of copper-gold ore. Nevertheless, the mine failed, and he died that same year at the age of 47. The old Chesterman property passed through a number of owners over the following decades, and was eventually acquired in the mid-1960s by Dr. Howard McDiarmid, the local physician and MLA who lobbied for the creation of Pacific Rim park. Over the following years, the McDiarmid family subdivided Chesterman's old pre-emption into the lots along Lynn Road, and built the landmark Wickaninnish Inn that overlooks the north end of Chesterman Beach.

Walter Guppy, a former prospector and author of several books on the area's history, arrived in Tofino as a young boy in 1921. His family moved into the old Chesterman home, which by then had been abandoned, and later lived in Tofino. He recalls how in those days, the old settlement across the water at Clayoquot was still an important part of the community's social life. On the May long weekend, an important annual sporting event called Clayoquot Days was held on the island. Natives, Norwegians, Scots and others poured in from all the settlements between Nootka Island and Ucluelet to gather for a weekend of competition and festivity, including boat-racing, long jump and tug-of-war events. The competitors—fishermen, farmers and loggers—were lean and muscular from the hard lives they led, and competition was tough.

An Opitsat man, Isaac Charlie, broke the world record for running broad jump, albeit unofficially. Walter himself remembers participating in Clayoquot Days competitions: "I was just a little shaver at that time, maybe eight or 10; or as a matter of fact I might have been a bit older because I remember rowing in a boat race in my brother Dick's skiff. The Indians used to come over, a lot of good athletes among the Indians. One event was only for Indians: the upset canoe races. They'd put two men in each canoe and at some point someone would fire a gun and they would have to tip the canoe, slosh the water out, and get back in and continue on their way."

In those days, of course, Tofino still had no road access to anywhere. All transportation was by boat, or on foot along the beaches to Ucluelet. The community was water-based, with settlers and homesteaders scattered about the islands on the harbour; Tofino itself might as well still have been an island. Clayoquot was the social centre, and Stockham Island also had a hotel and a store. The town cemetery was located on Morpheus Island. Funeral services were often disrupted by stormy weather that prevented people from wearing their fine clothes or from attending at all. Walter Guppy recalls: "There was a story that once they dropped a coffin overboard; the lifeboat took a roll or something, and the coffin slipped off. I don't know if that's really true or not, but on a stormy day it was pretty difficult . . ."

Arline Craig (née Bond) arrived with her family in 1921 as a young girl of four. They lived for five years on Stone Island, then moved to adjacent Nielson Island. She remembers rowing across to Tofino to attend the school there, a one-room school with a single teacher for about 20 children ranging in age from grades one through seven. That old schoolhouse later became the village office building on 3rd Street. Arline also recalls visits by Opitsat Natives to her island home. "We couldn't understand them in those days. They didn't speak much English. They would drop by our house, come in their big canoe. They would make a noise and Mom would come down and try to talk to them. She'd bring them a loaf of bread and they'd give her a fish. They were very friendly."

Above: Pioneer Arline Craig has lived on the shores of Tofino Harbour for over eighty years.

Left: Peaceful fishing at sunset, Lone Cone in background.

Lennard Island Light

The elegant lighthouse that marks the southern entrance to Clayoquot Sound commenced operation on November 1, 1904. Francis Garrard, the first keeper, moved out to the island during construction with his wife, six children, household effects, a cow and calf, a dog and cats, and they lived in the oil house until the dwelling house was constructed. When finished, Lennard Island was one of the most powerful lighthouses on the coast. Garrard's duties included pumping up the air tanks that pressurized the lamp and winding up the clockworks that rotated the light every two and a half hours, a task that had him sleeping in the lighthouse tower most nights. The following year the foghorn was constructed. It was run first by boilers, fired by both wood and coal, and later by diesel compressors. Construction of the foghorn meant a bit of company for the Garrard family, as more crew were required to run it.

In 2004 Lennard Island was one of 27 staffed lighthouses remaining on the BC coast, though it had lost its voice. For nearly a century the foghorn bellowed its mournful call once every minute whenever fog shrouded the coast. In the summer of 2003, it wailed its final call, victim of a new coast guard policy that mariners should rely on their own electronic navigation aids. Many of the long-term residents of Chesterman Beach now find strolling through the fog an eerily silent experience.

Elegant Lennard Island lighthouse marks the southern entrance to Clayoquot Sound.

The main event for the town was the arrival of the Canadian Pacific Railway steamship *Princess Maquinna* every 10 days as she journeyed up and down the coast from Victoria. Everyone who could walk would gather at the 1st Street dock, not because they were expecting company or freight, but because everyone else would be there, and gossip and news would be flying. It was the seaside town's equivalent of the Farmers' Market. The *Maquinna*, also known as Old Faithful, was as central to

life in Tofino as she was to Ucluelet and other isolated villages on Vancouver Island's outer coast.

During the 1920s, Japanese settlers arrived in Clayoquot. They were expert fishermen and brought the skill of salmon trolling to the area. Although relations were generally friendly, they settled in separate communities beside Tofino and Clayoquot. By 1923 there were about 30 Japanese families in the area, and they formed a significant part of the non-Native population. Japanese children attended the community schools, then went to special Japanese language schools after their regular classes.

Throughout the 1920s and '30s the Japanese settlers lived and worked in the area, and many friendships were formed. This changed abruptly after Japan bombed Pearl Harbor in December 1941: early in 1942 the Canadian government ordered all West Coast residents of Japanese descent to be removed. Their fishing boats were confiscated and they were sent to internment camps in the BC interior, the prairie provinces and Ontario. Within days, their homes and villages were deserted.

Tofino resident Islay MacLeod, who was a schoolchild in Tofino at the time, remembers how she felt: "Time seemed to stop for me that day in Tofino. There were my friends, Emiko and her sister Sachiko . . . and there was the Japanese boy who had

The Eagle Aerie Gallery (above) has become a Tofino landmark, thanks to the prodigious talents of First Nations artist Roy Henry Vickers (below).

91

In the old community cemetery on Morpheus Island, a mossy grave marker bears silent witness to Tofino's vanished Japanese community.

Pages 94-95: A cloud of western sandpipers and dunlin rises from the beach. Hundreds of thousands pause on their long migrations to feed in the Tofino area.

won a place in my heart forever by helping me with my Arithmetic. And there were all the others milling about me on the Government wharf . . . I had never seen so many Japanese adults and children together at one time. It seemed to my young eyes that half the population of Tofino was leaving. And there we were, the other half . . . watching, watching, watching . . . as our former friends gathered their pitifully few belongings together. These friends who almost overnight became our enemy . . . there was no communication between 'us' and our friends, who suddenly and to me, miraculously became 'the mistrusted alien Japanese'."

Although the Japanese Canadians were officially allowed to return in 1949, few came back to the West Coast. Those who did had to start over from scratch, as their homes and boats had been disposed of by the federal Custodian of Enemy Property. In Tofino itself, prejudice was rampant in the immediate post-war period. A resolution by the Tofino village commissioners on January 24, 1947, proclaims (illegally) that "all Orientals be excluded completely from this Municipality, and shall be prevented from owning property or carrying on business directly or indirectly within the Municipality." Today, no descendants of the Japanese settlers remain in Tofino, and only a handful reside in Ucluelet.

Through the 1950s and '60s, Tofino was a frontier town, sleepy and quaint to outside appearances, but still a bit rough around the edges. Fishing and logging were the main economic activities, and the Maquinna Hotel was a wild place by night.

By the late 1960s, hippies had started to migrate westward. Most squatted on Long Beach to the south and used Ucluelet as their base, but many headed north to Tofino after they were evicted from the newly created national park in 1971. Many of these former hippies still live in Tofino today. Some are short-haired and running conventional businesses, others are still long-haired and following alternative paths, but all are significantly greyer.

One who arrived about that time, and became a legend on Chesterman Beach, was the late Henry Nolla. A little too old to be a real hippie, Henry moved around for a decade or so, spending time at Long Beach, Tofino and Ucluelet. At one point, saddled with roommates who refused to wash their dishes, Henry set to carving each person a wooden bowl with a distinct design. He put some pegs in the wall, hid the china dishware in the woods and told them, "You can wash your own bowl and hang it up, or you can just hang it up."

Henry's bowls caught people's interest, and he began to receive requests for carvings. By this time the McDiarmid family had acquired the old Chesterman pre-emption, and Dr. McDiarmid asked Henry to stay on as caretaker at the north end of the beach, "just for a year or so."

Henry dedicated himself to a simple life, revolving around carving. He later apprenticed with Roy Henry Vickers, a talented Native artist from northern BC, and learned much about traditional Native designs. When the Wickaninnish Inn opened, more than 20 years after Henry started caretaking, he still lived in his little A-frame, and his adjacent carving shed had become a local icon and tourist attraction. With construction of the new Wickaninnish Inn addition in 2003, Henry finally had to move. He said: "That little cabin cost me $1,500 and two weeks' time. They said it was only for a year at most. I got nearly 29 years out of it. That's cheap rent!"

Henry was well loved in Tofino for his big heart, his open door and his simple philosophy toward life, which helped us all to keep things in perspective. "You get a carpet, then you gotta get a vacuum cleaner," he would say. "And then the dog can't come in."

(Above) Surfer in front of Long Beach Lodge.
(Below) Tofino surfer Raph Bruhwiler. **Jason Feaver**

Freshly caught geoduck clams await delivery on a Tofino dock.

Tofino is home to over 20 whale-watching operators such as this one, making a sighting off Vargas Island.

Shorebird Festival

Every year during the first week of May, tens of thousands of shorebirds congregate on the shores of the Esowista Peninsula. Ranging from the diminutive least sandpipers to larger birds such as whimbrels and greater yellowlegs, they stop on the beaches and mud flats on their annual migration northward to breeding grounds in the Arctic. Many fly non-stop from wintering grounds in California, Mexico and Central America to Clayoquot and lose up to half of their body weight during the long flight. The shores of Clayoquot are an important feeding ground for the birds: they stop here for a week or so, feeding and fattening up so that they can complete their flight north. Tofino locals vigorously protect their tiny feathered friends, celebrating their arrival with an annual Shorebird Festival and educating visitors about the importance of not disturbing the resting flocks.

Today, tourism is the mainstay of Tofino's economy. Only a decade ago, winter was a bleak period for Tofino locals. Restaurants and galleries closed. Those who had earned enough in their summer season to purchase airfare headed south; those who hadn't hunkered down in front of the wood stove. The opening of new luxury resorts has turned the town into a year-round destination. New businesses are appearing: galleries and restaurants and cafés and spas, and they remain open year-round. Locals can finally get "real" jobs.

Tofino: Geoduck Capital of Canada

The geoduck (pronounced "gooey-duck") is a type of large clam that lives on shallow, sandy, current-swept banks—habitat that is abundant in Clayoquot Sound. The average geoduck weighs about one kilogram, but individual clams can weigh more than five kilograms and can live as long as 168 years. They live under the sand, and feed using a giant siphon up to one metre long that extends up to the sea floor. This siphon is so large that the geoduck cannot retract it into its shell. It is estimated that the total weight of geoducks living in Clayoquot is over 56,000 tonnes. The fishery is carefully controlled, so that less than one percent of that weight is harvested annually, giving these long-lived clams enough time to procreate and grow—a sustainably managed fishery.

Local beaches offer a perfect promenade for mothers with baby strollers.

Even the smallest beach-combers have a natural fascination with intertidal life.

Opposite bottom:
Aspiring carvers appren-
ticed with the master at
Henry Nolla's old shed
beside the Wick.

Undeterred by wind and
surf, a jogger crosses
Chesterman Beach in
front of the Wickanin-
nish Inn.

Storm-watching at the Wick

The Wickaninnish Inn was a dream of the McDiarmid family for decades. Dr. Howard McDiarmid had worked as a bellhop at the Banff Springs Hotel to put himself through medical school. After acquiring the old Chesterman pre-emption, he dreamed of one day building a motel on the point at the north end of the beach. Back then, in the 1970s, the road to Tofino was still new, and not many tourists made the long journey out here. Building a motel seemed a risky venture in such a remote place.

Howard talked about his idea for two decades, until finally people were tired of hearing about it. His son Charles recalls: "We finally told him to either do it or shut up and quit talking about it." By then Howard was having second thoughts about the venture, so it was put to a family vote and Howard was outvoted four to one. By then Charles had experience working in high-end hotels across North America, and he upgraded the vision from a motel to a luxurious resort.

The Wickaninnish Inn opened to a full house in the summer of 1996 with Charles in charge. "Pickup trucks were leaving with carpenters, sawhorses and skill saws, and right behind them were the Mercedes pulling in," he says.

The design of the Inn, both inside and out, deliberately brings natural elements into the elegant setting. Inside, objects from nature such as driftwood and beach rock form part of the furniture and the decor. Outside, the main entry doors have been carved and giant timbers have been hand-adzed by the carver Henry Nolla and his son Mark. The work of local artists is featured throughout the Inn.

The Inn was planned "from the ground up" with winter storm-watching in mind. The McDiarmid family knew, from the many years that they had spent out at their cabin on the point, that the north end of Chesterman Beach is a prime spot for witnessing the fury of winter storms. All of the rooms have floor-to-ceiling windows angled for the best view over the ocean, and many have double soaker tubs looking out to sea. "Most people live in the city," says Charles. "A rainy day in the city is a pain in the neck. A rainy day here is magic, nature at its finest! Nature rules."

One quick way to check the pulse of Tofino's social life is to drop in at the Common Loaf Bakery. Tourists refer to it by its proper name, but to residents it is simply "the Bakery." Through the summer months it is a bustle of activity, avoided by most locals. Behind the counter, no fewer than half a dozen cooks and servers squeeze past one another, refilling trays of muffins, buns and pizza slices as fast as they are emptied, and serving a lineup that often extends right out the door. Crows perch on the eaves above, not too shy to dive-bomb the unwary in the hope of knocking a beach bun to the ground. The Bakery is *the* meeting place in town. At any given moment there may be a business meeting complete with laptops and cell phones taking place at one table, a frazzled mother with most of the town's four-year-olds at the next table, and a pot deal going down under

another table. The Bakery's notice board is the only place to find out what is really going on in town, from what is for sale to who is looking for a ride to who is in town and who is away. Many of the notices do not list phone numbers or contact details, but between a first name and good old small-town word of mouth, the messages seem always to get passed on.

Above: The Wickaninnish Inn made good use of local materials and local artisans like carver Henry Nolla.

Previous pages: A couple strolls Chesterman Beach at sunset with Frank Island in silhouette.

Above: The romance of the wild edge calls to all who seek something different from life.

Right: A surfer dude and his partner roll into town to check out the action.

The Bakery's popularity is due more to its special atmosphere than to any shortage of alternative watering holes. Tofino has many culinary delights to offer, having the highest ratio of restaurants per capita of any BC town. Visitors and locals alike may choose fine cuisine with an emphasis on fresh seafood at any number of restaurants; or sushi at the Inn at Tuff City; or casual fast food with a gourmet flair at Sobo's, the award-winning purple taco truck on the highway near Chesterman Beach.

The event that caused the most animated talk around the Bakery in the summer of 2003 took place in 1811. The *Tonquin* incident that had cast such a dark shadow over Clayoquot Sound in the 19th century came thundering back to centre stage when a local fisherman snagged a crab trap in Templar Channel. Rod Palm, a local diver and long-time *Tonquin* searcher, went down to investigate, and found a chunk of rusted iron protruding from the swirling sands at the bottom of the channel. Palm had been waiting for a piece of news like this for years. After notifying authorities, he raised the rusty find. It proved to be an anchor, and adhered to it were turquoise glass trading beads manufactured in the early 1800s, along with wood fragments

that turned out to be from a species of oak from the east coast of North America, where the *Tonquin* originated. These details indicated that the anchor almost certainly belonged to the *Tonquin*.

The task of locating the wreck of the *Tonquin* had obsessed underwater archaeologists for decades. Because of its antiquity, its colourful legend and its historical significance, more time had been spent speculating on and searching for its exact whereabouts than that of any other wreck on the West Coast. Many thought that it would be found farther north, but the anchor was found right where the Tla-o-qui-aht always said it should be. Tla-o-qui-aht oral history states that the *Tonquin* did not sink immediately after the explosion: rather, the stern blew off. The Natives returned in canoes and attempted to tow the ship toward their village of Echachist, but a stiff westerly breeze prevented them from making headway. So they turned and started to tow the ship eastward, to the shores of the small bay they call Tin Wis. While under tow, the damaged ship took on water and sank.

The position of the anchor, and the beads that were found with it, indicate that this anchor was on deck when the ship sank. It is believed that the ship itself rests relatively intact under the sands where the anchor was found. If that is so, it would be one of the most historic finds from the fur trade period. Over the coming years, archaeologists, local historians and Tla-o-qui-aht First Nations plan to join forces to recover and display more of the ship and its artifacts. Whether or not that occurs, the rediscovery of the *Tonquin* forms a satisfying bridge between the Clayoquot of today and its turbulent early history.

The cork board at the Common Loaf Bakery is Tofino's true information centre.

Rod Palm and Carl Martin admire an anchor believed to be from the *Tonquin*, the ship that Carl's Tla-o-qui-aht ancestors attacked in 1811.

6
The Islands
(Meares, Flores, Vargas)

Tofino is the staging point for travel to Clayoquot Sound proper. Wonders await: remote and expansive sand beaches fringed by luxuriant salal bushes and wind-beaten spruce forest, quiet rainforest walks, wolves and deer roaming freely. The Sound is surrounded by beautiful forested slopes, but most of the action is on the islands.

Ocean fog and blue sky meet at Vargas Island's outer shore.

Looking southeast from the peak of 730-m Lone Cone Mountain, old-growth forest forms a solid carpet down to Lemmens Inlet.

Low tide exposes an edge of Tofino's extensive eel-grass beds, critical habitat for many species.

You *can* get out there, but as in the days of old, travel is mainly by boat.

Ever since humans first inhabited Clayoquot, the sea has been their highway. Seafaring is in the air of this place. A landscape divided by inlets and choked with brush made it nearly impossible for the first people to travel on foot, so they were forced to take to the water. For millennia, this meant paddling a dugout canoe. Dugouts were also the preferred means of transport for the earliest white settlers and missionaries, first fitted out with oars, sometimes with sails, and finally with outboard motors. The first Europeans to arrive were sailors, and their first industry was a watery one: the maritime fur trade. Their second, commercial fishing, was equally salty. But it was not an easy place to navigate; such were the dangers and disasters that the outer coast became known as the Graveyard of the Pacific. In 1965 the Tofino historian George Nicholson counted 148 wrecks along the West Coast, and there have been more since.

Cars rule in the Tofino and Ucluelet of today, but among the islands of the Sound the old maritime culture still reigns supreme. Some island residents rarely get into a car or venture any farther inland than the bustle of Tofino itself. Aside from the main water-based Native villages—Opitsat, Ahousat and Hot Springs—there are people who live in anything from family homes on islands to floathomes to illegal cabins tucked away in the forest.

Many of the smaller islands near Tofino are still privately owned holdovers from homesteading days. The tiniest islets may have only one home each; some larger ones are communally owned and have several dwellings, some seasonal but others occupied year-round by couples and families. Most homes have solar panels or windmills to produce a bit of electricity, and some have generators as well, but for the most part they rely on wood stoves for heat, propane for cooking, and candles and oil or gas lamps for light.

Island children grow up with little television or other electronic diversions and spend a lot of time outdoors. Many are experienced boat operators by the time they are shedding their baby fat.

Marine Meadows

Tofino and adjacent islands are surrounded by broad drying shallows, giving rise to the saying: "Tofino is a big place at low tide." The 1,770-hectare Tofino Mudflat ranks among the top 10 most critical wetlands for migratory waterfowl on Canada's west coast. Rod Palm, a naturalist with Tofino's Strawberry Island Research Society, has lately turned his attention to the underwater portion of the shallows. These little-understood marine meadows are covered in eelgrass beds that provide habitat for numerous ocean species, including baby salmon, Pacific herring and Dungeness crab. One study estimates that nearly 70 percent of commercial fish species rely on eelgrass habitat during some part of their life cycle. Marine meadows also serve as critical feeding stops for migrating Brant geese and other dabbling waterfowl. Worldwide, one-seventh of the Earth's marine meadows have disappeared in the last decade, placing a premium on those, like Clayoquot's, that remain intact.

For some people, life on the water is literally "on the water." Floathouses are an intriguing part of the Sound's water culture. While not strictly legal, they are not really illegal either. Their numbers are inherently self-limiting because there are few sites where a floathome can be anchored with adequate protection from both the southeasterly storms of winter and the northwesterly gales of summer. Life on a floathouse is much like island life. However, while island dwellers must deal with West Coast tides—the water level can change as much as four metres in six hours, making it tough to wrestle those heavy propane tanks up the gangplank some summer afternoons—floathomes rise and fall with the tide. You always have level parking! The big fear for floathome dwellers, though, is sinking: a strong blow or heavy snowfall can tip the structure and start it on its journey to the bottom with all the residents' possessions.

Floathouse-dweller Pipot Dupuis expresses his solidarity with all things marine.

Boating is second nature to water dwellers Shallon and baby Infinity.

Pipot Dupuis has lived on the water here for over a decade. Originally from France, he ended up living on a sailboat at Tofino's 4th Street dock after sailing around the world for eight years. When live-aboards were deemed illegal at 4th Street, he moved to a floathouse anchored alongside another dock in Tofino. He has lived here with his wife and two children for five years; concerns about the health of the Tofino Mudflat, however, trigger increasing restrictions. Pipot considers floathome dwellers to be an "endangered species, like many other marine mammals." He is a pure ocean dweller who runs whale-watching boats for a living. "Sometimes I spend a week or more without touching land. I drive the boat home from work and walk along the dock to my floathouse. I don't go up the hill. I have no purpose up the hill."

A Floating Studio

Mark Hobson, a wildlife artist, paints from a floating studio anchored up an inlet in the heart of Meares Island. Every chance he gets, he flees from the hustle and bustle of Tofino to his floathome, where he is surrounded by the natural subjects that he captures in watercolours, acrylics and oils.

The most elusive of those who live on the water are the squatters. Usually holders of non-mainstream values, they live in cabins hidden in the forest, on remote islets

Below: Local author and artist Joanna Streetly at her floathouse anchored up one of Clayoquot's quiet inlets.

Bottom: A greenhouse occupies a raft alongside the floathouse.

and up secluded inlets. I lived this lifestyle for two years. Like so many, I was in search of a simpler life, hoping to escape the confines of social norms and expectations. I purchased a tiny cabin knowing that I had no legal title to the land. I commuted to Tofino by kayak, slipping quietly under the cedar fronds along the shoreline so as not to attract attention.

Life was hardest in winter, when storms could rage for days and trap me on my island. Things taken for granted in town, such as having heat in your home or getting to the doctor when you are sick, were sometimes impossible. More than once I swore that this was ridiculous and wondered what I was doing with my life, but then a few days later, paddling home in the slanted golden light of evening with porpoises rising beside me, I would remember why I was here.

If you are lucky enough to be invited to an island home for the night, the reasons for choosing such a life will be apparent enough. Lying in bed with the silhouettes of giant spruces framed by your window, you become aware of absolute silence. Free from the electric hum of modern homes, so familiar that you no longer even realize that it exists, you become aware of a profound calmness and tranquility. Suddenly this life makes a lot of sense.

Left: A cosy floathouse anchored in the sheltered waters of Lemmens Inlet.

Clayoquot artist Mark Hobson paints in his floating studio, surrounded by the subjects of his art.

Only by virtue of their natural inaccessibility do the large islands of Clayoquot Sound remain an immense, mostly pristine wilderness today. Until the 1980s, these islands—Meares, Vargas and Flores—were largely spared from logging simply because it was easier for logging companies to extend roads on the mainland than to barge heavy equipment over the water. But by the late 1970s, good old-growth wood was getting scarce and the ancient forests of Meares Island beckoned. Tofino locals had tolerated the whittling away of their forests over the years, but now, suddenly, clear-cutting was at their doorstep, threatening their most cherished landmark.

The imminent threat to Meares was a pivotal point in Tofino's history, and indeed, in British Columbia's history. Dozens of BC communities had faced similar challenges over the years, then shrugged and turned away. Up to that moment, the forest industry was king in BC, and if people sometimes grumbled about silty drinking water or ruined salmon runs, nobody actually stood in its way. But in Tofino in 1979, a small band of citizens *did* decide to stand in its way, and nothing has been the same since—for them, for Clayoquot, for BC or, especially, for the BC forest industry. It all began when Darlene Choquette noticed a few boatloads of loggers heading over to Meares Island. She asked them what they were doing, and they casually informed her that they were flagging points in the forest in preparation for logging. With a handful of Tofino locals, Darlene helped form the Friends of Clayoquot Sound and

In the winter of 1984–85, Meares Island protestors braved the cold and wet to save the island's old-growth trees. **Mark Hobson**

went about trying to halt the logging. After four years of letter-writing campaigns and meetings, the province announced a logging plan for Meares that was little changed from MacMillan Bloedel's initial proposal. The Friends realized that they needed to try a different tactic. Maureen Fraser, who now runs the Common Loaf Bakery, was one of those pioneer activists.

"We organized an Easter Festival in April 1984, with music, dance, crafts, slide shows," she says, "all of us brainstorming, combining these things in a way that I think was unusual because we made it as much a party as a political statement." This "party" has since become the role model for countless environmental protests worldwide.

The activists had informed the Tla-o-qui-aht First Nations of their actions and invited them to participate. Up until the festival, Tla-o-qui-aht had listened but had made no commitments. Then, at the celebration, elected Chief Moses Martin announced that Tla-o-qui-aht would declare Meares Island a tribal park. "You could have knocked us over with a feather," says Maureen, "because none of us knew this was coming. For the first time, we realized that this is going to go someplace, we are not just a group of hippies trying to do something. First Nations have solidly come into this issue. From that moment I thought, 'This could work.'"

Through the winter of 1984–85, Tla-o-qui-aht and other Tofino locals camped in the small bay on the southeastern tip of Meares Island where the logging giant

Mosses and ferns, nurse logs, berry bushes and giant trees are all part of the complex rainforest ecosystem.

A black bear waits patiently for a spawning salmon to swim by.

Trailing lichens and mosses play their part in the multi-layered complexity of the old-growth forest.

Below: The elusive western red-backed salamander abounds in coastal rain forests.

Bottom: Energetic lovers, banana slugs may copulate for three days straight.

MacMillan Bloedel intended to land its equipment. The Tla-o-qui-aht canoe carvers Chief Robert Martin Sr. and his sons Joe, Carl and Bill, joined by the local carver Henry Nolla, started working logs into traditional dugout canoes, asserting their traditional territorial rights and demonstrating their use of the forest.

The blockade was maintained long enough for the Tla-o-qui-aht to get a court injunction halting further logging pending settlement of their land claim. The Friends of Clayoquot Sound spearheaded more campaigns to protect more old growth, turning Clayoquot into a global environmental hot spot. Forest protection campaigns have since become commonplace and have saved millions of hectares of old-growth forest, putting the once-indomitable forest industry on the defensive in BC. Looking back, the wonder is that a small band of otherwise private folk in remote Clayoquot had the vision and the nerve to launch such a revolution.

Two decades after that winter of protest on Meares, no trees have been cut. The Tla-o-qui-aht have stood fast and the whole issue is waiting upon the resolution of land claim negotiations. The ancient old-growth forests of Meares Island—the majestic spruces that support the bulky nests of bald eagles, the tiny beetles and plump banana slugs that break down debris to fertilize the trees, all of the cougars and bears and deer and wolves and mink and the medley of smaller animals and birds—are still here.

The tangled growth of the rain forest makes hiking nearly impossible. However, each of Clayoquot's large islands has a trail. A brief water-taxi ride from Tofino will get travellers to Meares Island for a hike along the Big Tree Trail. You can walk for about a half-kilometre on a mossy boardwalk through one of the least disturbed temperate rain forests on the planet, and adventurous hikers can continue past the end of the boardwalk to do a five-kilometre loop along a muddy path that takes you past some of the world's largest cedar trees.

Entering the forest from the shore, the first thing you notice is the chill, even on the sunniest of days. The thick canopy protects the forest floor from heat and drying in summer and from frosts and high winds in winter, making it an equable environment for all of the creatures who make their home down there. Life is slow and quiet on the rain forest floor: slugs slither silently on their missions of recycling while salamanders and frogs spend hours or even days motionlessly awaiting an insect meal. The carpet of green—mosses, ferns and liverworts—grows slowly, changing imperceptibly year after year, a storehouse of moisture and nutrients protected from the elements by the arching canopy overhead.

The jewel-like Pacific tree frog is one of many wonders to be met in the rainforest.

Rainforest Secrets

- Contrary to popular belief, carpenter ants don't eat wood but excavate it for living space. One of the things they do with the space is keep herds of aphids, which they milk for their sweet fluid. They even take the aphids outside to graze in summer and tuck them back in the barn during winter.
- Vaux's swifts are swallow-like birds that fly through the dense rainforest canopy as fast as 60 km/h, snapping up insects. Though only 15 centimetres long, they prefer hollow snags a metre or more thick to nest in.
- The hearts of tiny rainforest shrews beat 800 times a minute and they have to eat non-stop, sometimes even tackling much larger frogs and slugs.
- The marbled murrelet is a robin-sized seabird seldom seen ashore (it has trouble walking), but it nests on thick, mossy limbs high up in old-growth trees, sometimes flying many miles inland to find a suitable site.
- Many more species live below ground in the rain forest than above ground. The weight of fungal mycelia alone may bulk up to five tonnes per hectare.
- The rain forest boasts many species of truffles. Nature makes them fragrant and tasty so that mammals will dig them up and spread their spores.
- The giant banana slug, a leading candidate for mascot of the coastal rain forest, measures up to 28 centimetres in length, and has a top recorded speed of .051 km/h. They are both male and female at the same time and don't need to mate to produce young, but like to whenever possible. They have homing instincts and tend to return to the same shelters to sleep.

The 10,000 years that have elapsed since the retreat of the giant ice sheets is not so long a time from the perspective of a 2,000-year-old cedar tree. From the Meares boardwalk there are numerous places where you can see just how little organic soil has built up on top of the clay and rock left bare by the glaciers. The soil is thin and poor; the few nutrients it contains get leached away by the abundant winter rains. It is a tough place for a baby tree to start its life. Fortunately, Mother Nature has a plan, and in the coastal temperate rain forest she has devised a special caregiver for her babies: the nurse log.

Under the protection of the rainforest canopy, fallen logs decompose slowly, rotting away over hundreds or even thousands of years. The decaying wood is like a soft orange sponge, moist and rich in nutrients and all sorts of micro-organisms, forming the ideal environment for a seedling to get a healthy start in life. As the sapling grows, its roots reach out, around and through the nurse log, eventually getting through to solid earth. The nurse log eventually rots away, and those roots strengthen to become the solid base of the tree.

I used to guide kayakers to Meares Island. Walking slowly under moss-draped

the wild edge

The bunchberry or dwarf dogwood produces clusters of bright red berries.

Tofino nature photographer Adrian Dorst working in the Vargas Island bog.

cedars, I would attempt to explain the logging issue. Many times one of my guests would gaze up in wonder at the hugeness, the incomprehensible immensity and complexity of this forest, and ask: "Why do they want to log here? Why don't they log somewhere else?" And I would have to explain sadly that the issue is not just about logging *here*. The "somewhere elses" were just the same, but they are gone now. What is special about Meares is that it is still here.

On Vargas Island, a five-kilometre trail starts at the Vargas Island Inn and crosses the rain forest and coastal bog to take you to spectacular Ahous Bay. Edged by a long, surf-dashed sandy beach, the bay is a summer feeding ground for gray whales, which can often be seen from shore. The Vargas Island bog is a good example of typical coastal bog: close to the edge of the ocean, it formed on flat lowlands underlain by sands that were left behind when sea level was just a few metres higher than it is now. Silica in the sand reacts with rainwater to create acid, and the peat moss that grows here produces even more acid. The result is a chemical environment too toxic for most forest species. Only plants like peat mosses, jack pines, shrubs such as poisonous bog laurel and Labrador tea, and some grasses can tolerate the conditions.

The Steller's jay, one of the rain forest's most outspoken residents.

The bog is also home to some unusual plants. The carnivorous sundew and butterwort both survive in the nutrient-poor bog water by fortifying themselves with insect meals. The sundew has delicate red hairs on its leaves, each with a honey-like drop at its end, enticing flies to come in for a lick. The sticky liquid traps the insects, and as they struggle to get free, they get stuck to more and more hairs, until the whole leaf curls around the unlucky bug and starts digesting it. Butterworts wrap their smooth, pale green leaves, which are coated with a sticky liquid, around any insects that drop by.

A bizarre rainforest organism, the slime mould straddles the border between plants and animals.

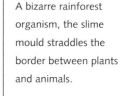

Following pages: A favoured feeding ground of gray whales, broad Ahous Bay on Vargas Island is the traditional home of the Ahousaht people.

115

The shimmering sands of Ahous Bay are sculpted into colourful stripes by wave action.

Neil and Marilyn Buckle live on Vargas Island. In the 1970s they bought the land that had originally been homesteaded by Neil's grandfather. With their hired hand Larry, they started a sawmill and built themselves a solid Tudor-style home from timber cut on the property. Carving a life in the wilderness and frequently visited by cougars, wolves and bears, they supported themselves and three sons. The boys are long gone, but Larry has stayed. Marilyn opened a B&B in the big house, but found it hard to adjust to living with so many people coming and going from her home. So she and Neil built themselves a smaller home down at the other end of the beach, and she now runs the Vargas Island Inn as a hostel. They survive on earnings from the hostel and the mill, supplemented with produce from Neil's vegetable garden behind the inn and the fresh crab and salmon that they catch virtually on their doorstep. Guests are sometimes surprised to find a bucket full of shellfish outside their door, courtesy of the hosts. Larry occasionally complains in his gruff voice about the stress, but in general life on Vargas is slow and mellow. Only five kilometres by boat from Tofino, it is a different world.

Above: Sea otters, hunted to extinction in BC two centuries ago, are now returning to the Clayoquot area. **Jason Feaver**

Far left: Neil and Marilyn Buckle run the Vargas Island Inn as a hostel.

Left: Neil Buckle crabbing on his doorstep.

The Return of the Sea Otter

Unless you are a commercial shell-fisher, one of the heartwarming stories of recent years has to be the recovery of West Coast sea otter populations. Before Captain Cook's crew discovered that Chinese mandarins would buy a sea otter hide for $300 (in 1778 dollars), touching off the marine fur trade, the cuddly critters were abundant along the entire coast from Alaska to California. By 1911, when they were protected by international convention, only about 2,000 animals remained, and the last BC sea otter was shot in 1929. Between 1969 and 1972, 89 animals were relocated from Alaska to northern Vancouver Island, and their population has been growing by about 20 percent a year ever since. In the summer of 2004, whale-watchers reported large rafts of sea otters outside Vargas Island, the first sightings that far south in over a century. The otter story is a continuing lesson in ecological linkages. Since otters' preferred diet is sea urchins, urchin populations exploded when the otter population dropped off. Urchins eat kelp, so the great kelp forests of early times disappeared. Now that the otters are back, urchin numbers are down and the kelp is coming back. The boom in otter numbers, however, has driven them in search of other foods such as Dungeness crab and geoduck clams, hence the ire of the fishermen.

Flores Island boasts the Wild Side trail. The trailhead is in the village of Ahousat, which visitors can reach by water taxi. Most of the trail follows wild, uninhabited beaches along the southern shores of Flores Island to Cow Bay, another of the gray whales' favourite feeding grounds, and along the way the trail crosses through short stretches of rain forest. From here it rises, twisting through thick rain forest, to the peak of Mount Flores, offering dazzling views of the ocean and islands to the south. To do this trail justice you should take a tent and camp out for at least two nights. Even if you have only one day, it is worthwhile if you leave early from Ahousat and go as far as you can before it is time to turn around.

For those who have the time and prefer to travel in silence, in tune with the changing winds and tides, kayaking is by far the best way to travel through Clayoquot Sound. Several touring companies in Tofino offer guided trips ranging in length from a few hours to a whole week. Experienced kayakers can rent boats and go for as long as they please—but beware! In summer the protected waters of Tofino harbour can appear to be a lake, but don't be fooled. Conditions can change abruptly: interactions between sudden winds and strong tidal currents can turn that "lake" into raging white water in a matter of minutes, and many of Clayoquot's waters are exposed to ocean swell, which can make landing or leaving beaches a dangerous exercise. If you are not an experienced rough-water ocean kayaker, paddle with a guide.

A western sandpiper dons its winter plumage.

Whale-watching and bear-watching tours are a great way to experience the islands and the wildlife for a day. The first gray whales arrive in March, and some stay in Clayoquot's waters until mid-fall. Humpback whales had all but disappeared from Clayoquot's waters until a few years ago, when they began to make a spectacular comeback. Chances are now good that you will see one during the summer months. The movements of the orcas are unpredictable, but there is a possibility of running into them at any time of the year. Bear-watching by boat is a relatively new activity in Clayoquot. Try to time your trip for early morning when the tide is low (usually just after the full or new moon), and you will have a really good chance of seeing bears up close: at those times they are most likely to descend to the sheltered shorelines, overturning rocks in search of crabs, barnacles and other marine delicacies.

Clayoquot Sound is one of the few places in the world where real wilderness lies literally at the doorstep. You don't have to hike for days to get away from it all: with a short boat ride, you are there. On photographing trips I am often gone for more than a week. On some trips I have the most amazing experiences with wildlife, and on others I see nothing. On those occasions I content myself with the peacefulness and power of the landscape. I feel sad when I talk to a tourist who, after spending a day on a boat cruising these spectacular waters, says to me: "But we didn't see a bear," or: "We never saw a whale." It is not a zoo, and even if you see wildlife, it will probably not be close up. For me, just knowing that they are there is enough.

The big islands are home to some of the most important Nuu-chah-nulth villages on the coast. The Tla-o-qui-aht village of Opitsat on Meares Island has about 150 residents, and has probably been occupied for 5,000 years or more. On Vargas Island, the village of Kelsemat was occupied until early last century, when a canoeing accident resulted in the death of many of the Kelsemaht tribe's men; the remaining Kelsemaht amalgamated with the powerful Ahousaht band on Flores Island. Home to about 750

Opposite top: The Wild Side Heritage Trail winds past spectacular Cow Bay on Flores Island, a popular stop for kayakers.

Opposite bottom: Looking west from Clayoquot Sound, the sun appears to dissolve into the distant ocean.

Following pages: A feeding humpback whale plunges skyward, its accordion-like throat swollen with tonnes of fish-laden water.
John Forde

people, Ahousat is one of the largest First Nations villages on the BC coast.

Life in these villages today is an intriguing juxtaposition of ways both old and new. Motorboats with powerful engines come and go constantly from the docks. Most families have satellite dishes ensconced in their yards and a minivan or car parked in Tofino for going "to town" (which means Port Alberni). They may also have a bag of freshly dug clams or a bucket of live urchins waving their spines set out by the back door, a bundle of newly stripped cedar bark awaiting cleaning on the porch, or the head of a deer hanging over the veranda.

Opitsat is only a five-minute boat ride from Tofino. Tla-o-qui-aht come across to do their grocery shopping and go to the post office. The children attend primary school in Tofino and travel by bus to Ucluelet for high school. Ahousat, on the other hand, has its own grocery store and post office, and many people operate small stores from their homes, offering smokes, snacks and fresh bread. Ahousat has its own school, and Hesquiaht students travel by boat from Hot Springs to attend the high school here.

Tla-o-qui-aht have a local newspaper to serve their two villages, Opitsat and Esowista at Long Beach. Newspapers are unnecessary in Ahousat: almost every home is fitted with a marine VHF radio. Everyone's radio is on all day, and it is used for everything—finding out when hubby will be home from fishing, handling a medical

One of Opitsat's famous beach cows feeds on seaweed in front of the village at low tide.

emergency, advertising community events and announcing that Rosie has bread for sale fresh out of the oven. Everyone knows everything about everyone, as it is happening, and this creates a great sense of community.

A stone's throw west of Opitsat, around the southwestern tip of Meares Island and just out of sight of Tofino, is Kakawis. The name Kakawis ("the place of many berries") seems innocent enough, but it makes many Nuu-chah-nulth shudder. Kakawis is the former site of the Christie Residential School. Opened in 1900, Christie was the dream of Father Augustin Joseph Brabant, a Benedictine missionary who arrived on the West Coast in 1875 and lived in Hesquiat for more than 30 years. One of 56 residential schools across Canada, the school was established to remove children from what church and government considered to be the backward environment of their homes and shape them into model modern citizens. Children aged only six or seven were uprooted from their families and taught English and Latin, Mexican dancing and judo, but they no longer learned how to prepare traditional medicines, produce seal oil, extract purple dye from a sea urchin or carve a canoe. They were beaten for speaking their own language, and soon many could no longer communicate with their own grandparents. It was an attempt to solve the "Indian problem" through cultural genocide.

The Frank girls of Opitsat put on a show for the camera.

Preceding pages: Canoe
gatherings involving
many coastal tribes are
part of a vibrant cultural
revival by First Nations.

Some of the schools degenerated into hellholes of physical and sexual abuse. In 2001 a man was awarded more than $200,000 damages for repeated sexual abuse that he suffered at Christie, and a former supervisor from the Port Alberni Residential School is now serving 11 years in jail for indecent assault. Many friends have told me of malnourishment, beatings and rape at Christie and Port Alberni. Many have in their family history records of aunties and uncles or older brothers and sisters who went to Kakawis and never returned. Some families were told that their children had died of tuberculosis or pneumonia, but in other cases they simply disappeared.

Mabel Sport is an elder from Hesquiat. She recalls a little girl in the next bed at Christie who died for lack of medical attention. "I was forced to sleep in the same bed with kids who were dying of tuberculosis. That was the Christie Residential School around 1942. They were trying to kill us off, and it nearly worked."

Christie closed its doors at Kakawis in 1973, but it operated for another decade in Tofino, where the Tin Wis Hotel now stands. Significantly, the old buildings at Kakawis went up in flames a few years after the school closed. Today Kakawis is a treatment centre, where entire families can go and work together to break the cycles of abuse and addiction that haunt them. Today, Kakawis is a place of hope.

After more than two centuries of colonization, oppression and catastrophic population loss, the last few decades have brought some hopeful change to the Nuu-chah-nulth. The population is on the rise and a cultural renaissance is taking place. Many tribes are implementing language programs, with books, CDs and courses

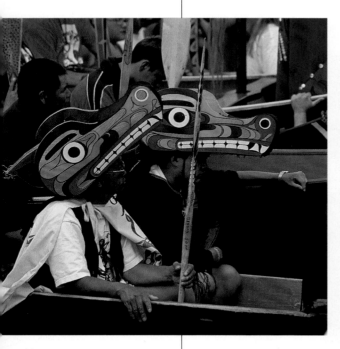

Above: Paddlers don traditional headdresses at a canoe event.

Right: Joe Martin (left) directs steaming of a new dugout canoe.

aimed at reviving the many local dialects that were so effectively eradicated by the nuns and priests. The once-banned potlatch ceremony is now taking place regularly, reaffirming family links and providing an opportunity to pass on traditions. Dugout canoes are reappearing up and down the coast and with them gatherings that strengthen cultural traditions and knowledge that, 20 years ago, were on the verge of disappearing. The canoes also create tourism opportunities, providing some Nuu-chah-nulth with income while maintaining their traditions. Last but not least, the Central Area tribes have formed a joint venture with the area's largest forest company, which will afford them a share of resource revenues at last, while allowing them to enforce environmentally sound forest practices.

Chief Alec Frank of Opitsat sports a traditional hat of woven red cedar bark.

The Canoe-Making Martin Brothers

For hundreds of years, Tla-o-qui-aht were famed as the carvers of the finest, most seaworthy canoes on Vancouver Island's outer coast. Now Joe, Carl and Bill Martin of Opitsat are restoring the tradition. The brothers had the good fortune to learn the ancient art from their grandfathers and their father, all traditional canoe makers. Although today they use power tools to speed the process, the methods and design that they employ are traditional and authentic. The outside of the hull is shaped, then the canoe is hollowed out. The prow and stern are attached as separate pieces. Finally the canoe is steamed and spread to add width, so that the finished vessel is wider than the log from which it was carved. The Martins trade their canoes with other tribes and even give them away at potlatches. They also teach canoe carving to tribes who have lost the art, inspiring young people with a sense of pride in their past.

Bill (left) and Carl Martin (light shirt) and helpers fit the prow piece on to a new dugout canoe in the boatshed at Opitsat.

7
The Wild North

T HE FAR NORTH OF
CLAYOQUOT, BEYOND
AND BEHIND THE ISLANDS, IS
SOME OF THE WILDEST AND
MOST REMOTE COUNTRY ON
VANCOUVER ISLAND. FROM THE
BOULDER BEACHES AND ROCKY
SHORES BETWEEN HOT SPRINGS
AND HESQUIAT, INLAND TO THE
HIGH ALPINE OF STRATHCONA,
THIS COUNTRY IS UNTAMED AND
SPARSELY POPULATED. IT IS HARD
TO GET TO. AND THAT IS WHY IT
IS STILL SO WILD.

Sydney Inlet glows with vibrant rainforest
colours on a calm morning. The inlet is
protected but the river valley beyond is slated
for logging.

A fault cuts a die-straight line across a sandstone shelf at Hesquiat.

Long, straight reefs at Siwash Cove, Flores Island, result from harder sandstone beds in the Hesquiat Formation.

North of Tofino, the nature of the coast transforms. The best way to see this is to hop on a float plane and head up toward Hot Springs. From the air over the outer coast of Vargas Island and on to the southern coast of Flores Island, the shoreline appears as a series of sweeping wave-laced beaches, punctuated by gnarled, sombre headlands of twisted black rock. Abruptly, about midway up the outer coast of Flores, things change. The shore turns to a low, boulder-strewn platform of wave-washed rock, scored by parallel lines marking the sedimentary beds of the Hesquiat Formation. The toughest of these sandstone beds make long, linear points that extend far out to sea as shallow rocky reefs. These submarine bars, Siwash Cove and Rafael Point on Flores Island, and Hesquiat Bar and Estevan Point farther north, throw up wild waves when seas are rough, and they are feared by navigators.

The sandstone and gravel beds of the Hesquiat Formation are unique on this part of the coast because they are the only rocks that were actually deposited here. Everything else—all the sedimentary and volcanic rocks underneath them—came from somewhere else, formed far out at sea and then carried to the coast by tectonic processes. Their collision with the continent pushed up mountains that started to erode about 35 million years ago. Great rivers washed sand, gravel and mud down the mountainsides, depositing layered beds in the shallow part of the ocean. Interlayered within the beds are fossils: shells of the snails and clams that lived in the shallow waters, and leaves and pieces of wood that indicate that the beds were deposited near to shore.

Little has happened, tectonically speaking, since the Hesquiat Formation was deposited. Although the beds have been faulted and tilted a bit, they have not been affected by the intense tectonic processes that formed mountains of the older rocks. Since the Hesquiat beds are much softer than the older rocks to the south and

Beds of sandstone and conglomerate erode into fantastic waveworn shapes in Hesquiat Harbour.

Above: A Nuu-chah-nulth family enjoys an outing to Hot Springs Cove.

Right: Kayaking into one of Hesquiat's many sea caves.

east, millennia of wave action have sculpted them into fantastic shapes—sweeping mounds, broad platforms and narrow chasms. Giant sea caves, huge caverns formed around the high-tide level, dot the coast between Hot Springs and Hesquiat Harbour. Many caves are sacred to the Nuu-chah-nulth people and have been used for burials for thousands of years.

Whether you are travelling north up the coast by boat or by float plane, Hot Springs Cove is the first stop of call after Flores Island. The cove, a safe harbour protected by the Openit Peninsula on its east side, has been used by Nuu-chah-nulth canoes for millennia, and by fishing boats for a century. The cove and peninsula, along with Sydney Inlet to the north and nearby parts of Flores Island, are the traditional territory of the Manhousaht, a small tribe that amalgamated with the Ahousaht tribe in years past. Hot Springs Village is now occupied by the Hesquiaht tribe, who live there with permission from the Manhousaht chief. In the village live a handful of families, about 100 people in all. They have an elementary school and a medical clinic staffed several days a week by doctors who drop in by float plane from Tofino.

Visitors arrive from all over to visit the natural hot springs at the tip of the Openit Peninsula. The springs are a 20-minute walk from the government docks on the east side of the cove, across from the village. The boardwalked trail is part of the whole Hot Springs experience. Its mossy slats are carved with the names of the many vessels—yachts from all over, as well as commercial fishing craft—that have anchored in the protected waters of the cove. Huge cedars shade the trail, their arching branches draped with old man's beard and licorice ferns. The undergrowth is a carpet of sword ferns and mosses, above which spread the giant shining leaves of skunk cabbage.

As you meander through the forest, the sudden whiff of sulphur wafting through the trees lets you know that you have arrived. From a narrow crack in the forest floor, water rises steaming and bubbling and cascades over a hot waterfall, to descend through a chain of tiny pools to the edge of the ocean. The temperatures of the pools change through the day with the movement of the tides. At low tide, the pools are steaming hot, becoming only slightly cooler as they drop toward the sea. As the tide rises, icy Pacific water surges into the lower pools with each wave. At the highest of tides, on a full moon or new moon, even the highest pool may be dashed by surf, icily cold and violently inaccessible. On most days, though, you can almost always find one pool that is just right.

Sun-tinted steam rises from the hot pools of Hot Springs Cove in Maquinna Marine Park, 37 km northwest of Tofino.

Anchored by the government docks is the *Innchanter*. Built in 1927, this 26-metre wooden freighter started its life as the *Burnaco*. It served the West Coast until just a few years ago, when Shaun Shelongosky bought it, rechristened it and fitted it out as a bed and breakfast that sleeps up to 12 people. The grand salon, finished in wood with accents in a nautical shade of blue, has a large dining room table as well as comfy couches and chairs nestled around the fireplace. As much as I love camping, the *Innchanter* is my favourite way to enjoy Hot Springs Cove. With a solid roof over my head, the wood fire crackling and Shaun's culinary delights to enjoy, it is the perfect base for a relaxing stay at Hot Springs.

Access to Hot Springs Cove is only by water or by air. The *Matlahaw* water taxi operates year-round, except on the stormiest of winter days. Whale-watching tours to the springs leave from Tofino daily, from spring through early fall, and float planes travel as weather permits.

The coast north of Hot Springs toward Hesquiat is rugged and exposed: sea cliffs and inclined boulder beaches are slammed by steep, dumping waves and fringed by dangerous rocky reefs. Hesquiat Harbour, a broad, open bay, is guarded at its mouth by the infamous Hesquiat Bar, a rocky wave-washed shoal. At the harbour's west entrance is the ancient village of Hesquiat (population 5), and at the head of the

Below: *Innchanter* owner Shaun Shelongosky is renowned for his culinary feats.

Right: The grand salon of the MV *Innchanter*, a floating 12-person B&B anchored in Hot Springs Cove.

harbour is Boat Basin (population 1). This is as remote as it gets: other than a few commercial fishers and the occasional hard-core surfer, few people visit Hesquiat. It is nearly impossible to get here! No scheduled water taxis serve the region, and only on a rare windless day can float planes land on the harbour.

As an experienced kayaker and former guide, I have paddled this stretch of coast several times. Each time I have found myself faced with a different challenge that has pushed me to my limits. On my first trip, on a sunny and relatively calm summer day, a thick fog bank suddenly engulfed me, testing my compass skills as I paddled blind, struggling to locate by sound alone the features on the nautical chart: rocky headlands, gently sloping sand beaches and steep boulder beaches. My heart was in my throat as I attempted to identify menacing shallow reefs, over which dangerous waves could suddenly break and swamp me, only by the feel of the swell passing under me. Getting to shore that day, landing through breaking surf at a beach I could not see, was one of the toughest experiences I have had in a kayak.

The sea caves and jagged rock formations of the coast between Hot Springs and Hesquiat Harbour are fascinating but difficult to explore.

Rafts of bull kelp are only one of the challenges kayakers face traversing Hesquiat's storm-prone shores.

Black bears are commonly seen on Hesquiat shores for most of the year, feeding on berries and grass and digging through washed-up seaweed for sand fleas.

On my second trip, after being trapped at Hesquiat Point for five days by an out-of-season storm, I put a hole in my boat while launching from a boulder beach in steep, dumping surf, and I was forced to bail while paddling my way back to Hot Springs. A few years later, as I headed up the coast with a friend, brisk summer gales hurled breaking waves in our faces, making for a long, rough paddle upcoast. When we finally arrived in the somewhat sheltered waters of the harbour, cold and wet and exhausted, we found every possible landing site patrolled by bears. Only at dark did we finally find a beach that appeared to be bear-free where we could put on some tea, shed our wet clothes and set up camp.

No one but the most experienced of paddlers should attempt to kayak this part of the coast. Advanced surf skills are needed on these beaches, even on the calmest days. On many days, landing a kayak anywhere on this coast is impossible (at least in one piece!). Both wind and wave conditions change rapidly, and big surf can trap you on a beach for days. The area is out of range of radios and cell phones, so rescue is unlikely. You are on your own.

The Hesquiat Peninsula, a broad, flat tongue of land protruding seaward from Vancouver Island's west coast, marks the farthest northerly reach of Clayoquot Sound. Low, rocky reefs in the nearshore waters focus giant curling waves into clean breaks that draw the toughest of the area's cold-water surfers. At the same time, these hazardous reefs keep most boats far from shore, preventing most visitors from approaching the wild peninsula. Only the occasional hikers pass through, walking in from Nootka Sound in the north. Carefully timing their passages to cross the rock shelves at low tide, they share their path with the bears and wolves that roam this wild land.

Hesquiat was the site of the very first contact between Europeans and Nuu-chah-nulth people. Four years before the arrival of Captain Cook, the Spanish explorer Juan Pérez was sailing southward in the ship *Santiago* on his return from a voyage intended to "examine the coast as far north as 60 degrees latitude." Needing to replenish its water supply, the *Santiago* anchored on the west side of the Hesquiat Peninsula on August 8, 1774.

Several hundred Hesquiaht were camped at a temporary fishing village. At around noon they noticed sails appearing on the horizon like some strange cloud. Through the afternoon, they watched the sails approach, and tension mounted in the village. Some people reacted with fear and hid in the woods; others climbed trees for a better view; medicine men donned headdresses, dancing and shaking rattles to stave off evil spirits.

The ship finally arrived, anchored and dropped its sails. The bravest of the Natives approached—21 canoes carrying 150 people in all. To them, the ship appeared to be a big floating house, and they thought they could recognize the deathly pale spirits of their ancestors walking about on the house. The Natives sang and shouted to make these ghosts go away.

A few brave Hesquiaht boarded the ship, and a handful of goods were traded. The first contact between Europeans and Nuu-chah-nulth people had been made. From this encounter, the Natives gave all "white" people the name that is still used for them today: *mamalthni*, which means "people who live on the water."

The Spaniards remained in the cove for the night. In the early morning a brisk west wind came up, and the ship started to drag anchor. The Spaniards sailed off, never actually having set foot on Vancouver Island.

A few years later and only a few miles to the north, Captain James Cook and his crew sailed into Nootka Sound and established contact with the next tribe to the north, the Mowachaht, under the chieftainship of Maquinna. From this meeting ensued a century of contact and trading between the West Coast tribes and visitors from Spain, England and America. Then, in 1875, the first European came to live with the Hesquiaht.

Fathers Charles Seghers and Augustin J. Brabant visited Hesquiat village in 1874. Finding it a central spot on the coast, and "the Indians of the best good will," they chose the spot to establish the first Catholic mission in the region. They returned the following year and built a small church and a priest's residence.

Brabant was placed in charge of the mission. Upon his arrival, he taught himself Chinook, the trading language that was used for intertribal conversation, and later he became fluent in the Hesquiaht language as well. Brabant ministered to the Natives over a huge area, from Barkley Sound in the south, to Clayoquot Sound and Hesquiat, to Nootka Sound in the north, mostly travelling by dugout canoe. He brought with him a bull and several cows, which started a wild herd that became infamous for their roamings on the Hesquiat Peninsula for many years. Father Brabant remained at Hesquiat for more than 30 years, until he was replaced by Reverend Charles Moser in 1910.

Looking across sheltered Hot Springs Cove toward Hot Springs Village from the government wharf. The Hesquiaht village was relocated from Hesquiat Harbour in the 1950s.

139

Only a few years after Father Brabant's departure, a new settler soon to become a legend arrived at Hesquiat. Ada Annie Rae-Arthur was born in California, had been educated overseas and then worked alongside her father on his newly purchased farm in northern Alberta. She learned much about hard work and about making a living in a tough place, and one of the skills she learned was how to handle a rifle.

In 1915, at the age of 27, Ada Annie arrived at Hesquiat with her husband Willie and their three young children. They had a pre-emption of 64 hectares at Boat Basin, on the south-facing slopes at the back of the harbour. The couple set out to create a farm from the rain forest, and to raise their family in the wilderness.

Ada Annie is now famous as Cougar Annie. She lived in Boat Basin for nearly 70 years, leaving only rarely for a quick visit to Tofino, and even more rarely for any more distant destination. Cougar Annie raised her eight children at Boat Basin, working her way through four husbands in the process. Bit by bit she carved a garden out of the rain forest, operating a successful mail-order flower bulb nursery as well as running Hesquiat's first post office. Her skill with the rifle came in handy when she had to defend her little farm against the wild animals that crowded in. She is reputed to have killed more than 70 cougars in her years at Hesquiat. She finally left her beloved homestead in 1983, blind and a semi-invalid, and died in Port Alberni hospital just short of her 97th birthday. Her garden has been restored by her old friend Peter Buckland, who purchased the property from her in 1981, and is now open to tourists who visit from Tofino, arriving by float plane or motorboat.

During the World War II years, numerous fears arose about Tofino's location on the West Coast, which exposed it to possible attack by Japan. The fears appeared to be justified in June 1942, when Estevan Lighthouse was shelled by a Japanese submarine,

Top: Visitors explore Cougar Annie's garden.

Above: View from 30-metre high Estevan Lighthouse, a towering landmark on the low-lying Hesquiat coast.

catapulting Hesquiat into the wartime headlines. Like so many tales from the coast, different versions of the story abound. Cougar Annie claimed to have seen the submarine surface in Hesquiat Harbour before the bombing took place and to have phoned the lighthouse to warn them, but the written account of E.T. Redford, the wireless operator at Estevan Point, makes no mention of her call.

Some shells passed over the lighthouse and landed clear on the other side of the peninsula, at the back of Hesquiat village. (Cougar Annie even claimed that one landed on her beach, 15 kilometres from the lighthouse.) Bernard Charleson is Hesquiaht, and he remembers his parents talking about it. "It was late evening. They didn't know what it was; they heard bombs going over the house and explosions." Bernard chuckles as he continues in his soft voice: "They didn't realize it was a submarine. They wouldn't have gone in boats if they had known it was a submarine! Those who had boats escaped, in canoes, rowboats and little putt-putts, and the rest ran into the bush. They went in their boats to Rae Basin (at the far end of the harbour) and hid in the bush there for days. They knew the war was on, but they didn't ever expect any bombing." Bernard even recalls finding Japanese mines, "the kind with the metal spikes sticking out," washed up on the beaches around Hesquiat for 15 or 20 years after the war.

Today the forest has swallowed many of the signs of Hesquiat's past. The gently curving beach where hundreds of Hesquiaht once lived and where Father Brabant ran his mission for more than 30 years is nearly abandoned. Most of the tribe moved to the safer harbour at Hot Springs Cove half a century ago. Berry bushes have overtaken the clearings that were once occupied by longhouses and the tiny church. Only one Hesquiaht family, headed by Dave and Diane Ignace, remains at the old village, collecting traditional seafoods, tending a vegetable patch and sporadically venturing to the outside world for supplies. In winter they are often stormbound for weeks at a time. In summer their relatives join them, and the beaches echo with laughter as in centuries past, as children splash around in the surf. The Ignace family soaks up the sun and tries to extract a year's worth of socializing from a few months.

Inland from Hesquiat and behind the big islands, craggy snow-capped mountain peaks rise as a glistening backdrop to Clayoquot Sound. Rivers fall from Vancouver Island's lofty centre: the Bedwell, the Atleo, the Cypre, the Moyeha, the Megin and the Sydney. In summer they are a series of sleepy pools shaded by majestic spruce trees, separated by shallow gravel bars that are smacked by blinding sunlight. Baby salmon dart like minnows through the crystal-clear water, waiting for autumn rains to link their pools to the sea. In winter, the waters rise to become boiling storm-fed cascades, bouncing branches and even entire logs down to the sea. Mossy bear trails fringe the banks, the products of millennia as generations of padded feet follow the paths of their ancestors.

Relics left by Cougar Annie Rae-Arthur, who spent 70 years in Boat Basin, raising eight children, burying four husbands and killing over 70 cougars.

The Bedwell River, behind Meares Island, is flanked by forested slopes, but the valley bottom itself was logged out decades ago. Giant stumps, as big as queen-size beds, now form nurse logs that support a clump of straggling saplings, all bolting skyward as they compete for light. The Atleo and the Cypre have fared even worse: the entire valleys have been logged. The slopes above the rivers are denuded, and the rivers themselves are filled with logging debris that has diminished their salmon runs. Stumps block the river mouths and silt chokes the gravel spawning beds. But the other large valleys behind Flores Island—the Moyeha, the Megin and the Sydney—are still untouched.

The Moyeha River valley is protected as part of Strathcona Provincial Park. It rises from Herbert Inlet to the east of Flores Island, a velvety green furrow that cuts into the heart of Vancouver Island, leading up to the high country. The river mouth is hard to get to, even by boat. Rarely visited by people, unscathed by so much as a hiking trail and home to creatures that have never laid eyes on a human being, this valley is truly a pristine fragment of wilderness virtually untouched by human hands.

The upper Megin River falls from rocky high country into Megin Lake. Bordered by steep mountain slopes cloaked in ancient hemlock and Douglas fir, the lake glistens

The Estevan light station is a remote and lonely place.

142

like a mirrored jewel embedded in the valley floor. From the lake's west end, the lower Megin River curves southward and meanders through small, rocky canyons and over broad gravel bars. Bigleaf maples, rare in the rest of Clayoquot, shade the Megin's bank in summer with their mossy branches and light up the valley with colour in the fall. The river tumbles into Shelter Inlet, a protected fjord behind Flores Island, through a narrow twisting gash cut into the rock.

The Megin valley is one of my favourite places. It is a challenge to get to, like most of the wild north. Hiking up it is hard work: you have to follow bear trails that suddenly disappear in thickets of thorny berry bushes or devil's club. I have never actually got very far on foot in the Megin valley, but the abundant red and yellow salmonberries and dangling clusters of huckleberries at least provide some compensation for the lack of progress on the ground.

Kayaking through the gap at the river mouth is tricky. At high tide the water passes sluggishly through, but at low tide the gap becomes a constricted waterfall with a drop of several metres. Paddling into the river at low tide is impossible, and paddling downstream at low tide is downright dangerous, presenting rock-studded curves before the precipitous drop. Only during the driest days of summer can you work your way upstream, entering the river mouth at high tide, then paddling up through the deep pools and dragging the kayak upstream over the gravelly shallows between them. The river floods rapidly in a heavy rain. I once found myself trapped up at the lake for a week with only a two-day supply of food, as the first autumn rains raised the riverbanks well into the forest and kept the white water gushing at flood levels.

Wolves are common visitors to the rocky shores of the Hesquiat Peninsula.

The headwaters of the Bedwell, the Moyeha and the Megin converge in the southwestern corner of Strathcona Provincial Park. Created in 1911, Strathcona is BC's oldest park and the largest park on Vancouver Island. Smack in the middle of the Island, it covers the high country, the source of rivers flowing southwestward into Barkley, Clayoquot and Nootka sounds, as well as rivers that flow eastward to Vancouver Island's protected inner shores, from Sayward to Campbell River to Comox.

Visible from much of the salt waters of Clayoquot Sound, the peaks of Strathcona rise to heights of over 2,000 metres. In winter this alpine environment consists of ice-encrusted crests and windswept snow. Even in summer, glaciers shroud the highest summits, as receding snow reveals delicate carpets of moss and stunted berry bushes for a brief growing season. Canada's highest waterfall, Della Falls, tumbles in a 440-metre freefall over a rocky precipice to the valley below. This delicate highland of glacier and tundra, although supposedly protected, has a checkered history. For a time commercial mining was allowed within the park, and to this day there is still one operating mine within park boundaries.

The Megin holds a special place in the hearts of many Tofino residents. It was nearly lost in April 1988, when British Columbia Forest Products started to build a road from the already logged-out Atleo River valley northward through Sulphur Passage in order to access the Megin. By chance, the Tofino photographer and artist Adrian Dorst was passing by Sulphur Passage in his Zodiac and heard a blast. He hurried back to Tofino and spread the alarm through the environmentalism community.

Those Controversial Fish Farms

Salmon farming is the most contentious new industry on the West Coast, and in 2004 Clayoquot Sound had 23 licensed sites, giving it one of the highest fish farming densities in BC. Proponents claim that fin-fish aquaculture is an environmentally friendly industry, but critics disagree. They point out that salmon farms are highly polluting. It is estimated the sites currently operating in Clayoquot produce as much raw sewage as a city of 100,000 people. There have also been problems with farmed fish escaping into the wild, where the Atlantic salmon raised in most farms pose a danger to the indigenous Pacific stocks. The open-net cages used attract predators, especially sea lions and seals, which farmers are licensed to kill. In the spring of 2001, a mass grave containing at least 15 sea lions killed by a farm operator was discovered in Clayoquot Sound, and in the last decade, BC farmers have reported killing 5,000 seals and sea lions. Farms also degrade scenic values and obstruct recreational use of the foreshore, especially in choice locations like Sulphur Passage Marine Park, where one company started a farm. However these issues are resolved, it is questionable whether salmon farming represents the best use of the resources in a natural area like Clayoquot.

Kayakers pass over rocky shallows in the Megin River, which was added to Strathcona Provincial Park after the Sulphur Passage blockades of 1988.

The Friends of Clayoquot Sound sprang into action. Although still weary from their limited success at Meares Island, they felt that they had no choice but to do their best for the Megin. It was one of the very few major watersheds left on Vancouver Island that was still completely untouched by logging.

Left: Della Falls, in Strathcona Provincial Park, is Canada's highest waterfall.

Below: Enchanting Sulphur Passage was made a marine park, but the fish farm stayed.

Bedwell Sound and the Bedwell River valley in winter, with peaks of Strathcona beyond.

From June through August 1988, FOCS members blockaded the road at Sulphur Passage. They placed themselves before advancing road-building machinery, at times risking their lives by sitting in the path of blast rock, above operating drills or in the trees above the work area. This time they were successful: the Megin River valley was protected as a 27,390-hectare addition to Strathcona Park in 1995.

Sydney Inlet, which reaches farther north than any other Clayoquot waterway, appears to have been sliced from the verdant hillsides with a knife. Velvety slopes of impenetrable rain forest drop from the hilltops straight to the sea. The nearly vertical shoreline prohibits landing from any watercraft, even a kayak. At the head of the inlet, the Sydney River debouches into an estuarine meadow dotted with chocolate lilies and bright red Indian paintbrush. The river follows a serpentine path up this dark and mysterious valley, far from any human settlements. In summer the river is a string of shady pools lined with clean pebbles that have been tumbled and polished by the violent cascade of winter-storm flood waters. I think the Sydney's foreboding character comes from its spruce trees, rising tall and dark and brooding. In the summer of 2003, the Canadian singer-songwriter Sarah McLachlan climbed one of these trees to bring attention to the fact that although Sydney Inlet is protected, the precious river valley is not. The Sydney may well become Clayoquot's next main battleground.

Rainforest Facts
- Temperate rain forests originally comprised less than .2 percent of the earth's land surface.
- About one-half (55 percent) of the world's temperate rain forest has been cut already.
- BC has about one-fourth of the world's remaining coastal temperate rain forest.
- About one-half (53 percent) of BC's coastal temperate rain forest has been cut already.
- Only 5.7 percent of Vancouver Island's temperate rain forest is protected.
- Clayoquot Sound has the largest tract of temperate rain forest and the largest cluster of unlogged valleys remaining on Vancouver Island, and has the only pristine rain forest on the island large enough to sustain fully functioning ecosystems.
- Of 102 valleys 5,000 hectares or larger on Vancouver Island, only 17 remain less than 2 percent logged.
- Six of these large intact valleys are in Clayoquot Sound.
- Two of them are protected: Megin and Moyeha (in Strathcona Provincial Park).
- Four of them are not protected: Sydney, Ursus, Bulson, Clayoquot.
- The two largest undeveloped islands off Vancouver Island are also in Clayoquot Sound: Flores and Meares.

The alpine of Strathcona is spectacular country, but very hard to get to. For those already in Tofino who want to experience Strathcona, I suggest a floatplane tour. Fifteen minutes from Tofino Harbour, you will be soaring over the craggy peaks and glistening glaciers, and you can get amazing views of Della Falls. Those who want to experience the park first-hand must drive almost full circle to get in: back east across the island, north to Campbell River, then west again and then south, into the heart

of the park at the south end of Buttle Lake. From here, seven marked hiking trails begin, as well as several short interpretive nature walks.

Getting into the wild north of Clayoquot is hard work, and of that I am glad. Hardly anyone goes there, and that is what keeps it so wild. Everywhere we humans go, we have an impact, no matter how gently we tread.

I have paddled with whales and sea otters in the turbulent waters beyond Hot Springs. I have watched a pack of wolves scurry and play on wide, rocky platforms along the outer Hesquiat Peninsula, and then heard them howling to one another in the forest as my companions and I hiked past. I have sat on the water's edge at the Megin River, cooking my breakfast as a big black bear padded past me, uninterested, on his usual morning route. I have been mesmerized by tiny alpine flowers and played in patches of snow in midsummer in Strathcona. I have been a part of the magic.

I venture into the wilds of the north carefully, slowly, gently, trying to respect the plants and wild creatures that live there. But I know that my presence, too, has an impact. I know how lucky I am to have experienced Clayoquot's wild north. And that is why I take these pictures—to give to those who may never see these wild lands first-hand, a touch of the magic.

I take a contemplative break while working my way up the Bedwell River valley into Strathcona Park.

8
Balance

Like millions of others, I first experienced the Clayoquot area as a tourist. I was impressed by the strength and the energy of this land, the timelessness and serenity of the rain forest, the roar of winter swell exploding on the rocks. But now, a tourist no more, I see more deeply. And what touches me most is no longer the strength of this place but rather its fragility.

This giant cedar tree was already ancient when the first Europeans came to the West Coast in 1774.

Previous pages: Aptly named Pretty Girl Cove, perhaps the only place on the BC coast you could view from this altitude and see nothing but virgin rain forest. Plans are to log it.

Opposite top: Environmentalists demonstrate to show Clayoquot is still being logged, despite its designation as a Biosphere Reserve.

Clear-cut logging advances near the Bedwell River mouth, as in many parts of Clayoquot.

On the scale of a human lifetime, this magnificent landscape seems ancient and timeless, and to us, change is imperceptible. But imagine an ancient cedar tree, one of those old Meares Island giants draped with pale cascades of old man's beard and plumed with licorice ferns, standing serenely in the rain forest. To the cedar tree, the giant ice sheets of the last ice age only disappeared five lifetimes ago. It has seen the shorelines shift as the seas rise and fall. The last huge, subduction-related megathrust earthquake that shook this coast occurred before recorded history—but that cedar tree has experienced *three* of them. And it was already an ancient giant, probably little different than it is today, when the Hesquiaht, fishing peacefully one summer from a little wave-washed cove, first laid eyes on the pale bearded men who sailed in from the sea.

Imagine now a cedar cone falling down from the canopy, alighting on a mossy log and shaking loose a seed. It plunges its roots deep into the damp decay of a spongy old nurse log, a moist source of nutrients that will sustain the young tree for the next few hundreds of years. What will this cedar tree see in its lifetime? Will it see the last generation of salmon wash down the streams to the sea, never to return again? Will it see the last pack of wolves slipping through the forest, hungry and desperate as habitat and food sources disappear? Will it see the forest fall away around it, until one day it feels the bite of the chainsaw on its own skin?

In the summer of 2004, people in Tofino were celebrating because Interfor, the forest company that owns the cutting rights to Sulphur Passage and the Sydney

watershed, agreed to postpone logging for five years. But five years and even 50 years are nothing on the scale we must conceive if we truly wish to guarantee that cedar seedling safe passage through all the stages of its life cycle.

I view the matter in terms of balance and equilibrium. Safeguarding that old grandmother cedar through the stages of her long life requires a sustained state of balance and equilibrium uncommon in the recent life of our planet. The ending of the ice age produced a great disequilibrium. During those first millennia following the retreat of the great ice sheets, change was the only constant as the climate warmed and new species arrived, including western red cedar. Equilibrium was only attained when the first great cedar logs on the forest floor finally decayed to nothing. By that time, Nuu-chah-nulth culture had also reached a climax or equilibrium state. Their use of the resources was limited to their own needs, and their population was limited by the availability of the resources.

With the arrival of the Europeans, equilibrium was broken. Resources were extracted and sent to markets overseas. The first victim was the sea otter, a survivor on this coast for untold millennia that was hunted to local extinction within a generation. Next came Captain Stamp with his sawmill, and within a century, three-quarters of the productive rain forest on Vancouver Island had been cut. Other casualties were the fur seals, the humpback whales and the herring. Equilibrium has been lost, and it is obvious to anyone who thinks about it that things can't go on in this way if future generations are to inherit a livable world.

Most thoughtful people are aware of this and trust that those responsible will eventually do what needs to be done. The vision that set the defenders of Clayoquot apart is the fear that by the time all the polite debates over sustainable forestry are exhausted, the last ancient cedar on Meares will have been cut and the great struggle will have been lost by default. As Klaus Toepfer, executive director of the UN Environment Programs, said in 2000, "Short of a miraculous transformation in the attitude of people and governments, the Earth's remaining closed-canopy forests and their associated biodiversity are destined to disappear in the coming decades."

Toepfer continued, "Knowing it is unlikely that all forests can be protected, it would be better to focus conservation priorities on those target areas that have the best prospects for continued existence." It is this simple principle that underlies the effort to save Clayoquot. No matter how or when the jobs-versus-environment debate is resolved, we will need some intact examples of major ecosystems like the temperate rain forest to study, to admire and to serve as refugia for all the biodiversity needed to repopulate the vast areas "disturbed" by industry, just like the refugia that restocked the coast after the ice age. You do not have to become a convert to the no-growth

In 2003, recording artist Sarah McLachlan climbed one of the Sydney Valley's towering spruce trees to bring attention to the threat posed by logging.

economy to recognize the folly of destroying the last working example of anything. Nor should it be difficult for the most pragmatic person to agree that if such a refuge is to do its job, it must be a self-sufficient working model. It will be little use if its key ecological systems are compromised in ways that will cause the interconnected whole to collapse after a few generations or a few centuries. This is why major wilderness preserves like Clayoquot cannot be hacked up. They must have critical mass.

So what is the status of Clayoquot after two decades of conservationist effort? Following the pioneering Meares Island campaign that started in 1979, logging was halted, but neither Meares nor Flores Island is formally protected. Both are still included in active Tree Farm Licences, and only the court ruling that Tla-o-qui-aht land claims must first be settled prevents logging from resuming legally on Meares. The campaign to save the Megin River valley in 1988 succeeded in that the watershed was added to Strathcona Park, but many nearby areas of old growth are still endangered.

Top: Environmentalists spread their message.

Above: Small-patch logging near the mouth of the Moyeha River, an innovation of the Clayoquot Scientific Panel, is an improvement over massive clear-cuts of the past.

In 1993 the BC government announced a plan to protect 33 percent of Clayoquot, leaving most of the rest (62% of the whole) open to logging, including the Clayoquot, Ursus and Sydney River valleys, Easter Lake and Flores Island. (It is significant that much of the "protected" area consists of coastal bog and other areas that are unsuitable for logging anyway.) The 1993 blockade of the Kennedy River bridge brought logging to a halt and spurred the government to establish the Scientific Panel for Sustainable Forest Practices in Clayoquot Sound. In 1995 the government accepted all of the panel's 120-plus recommendations calling for, among other things, ecosystem-based forest management, the elimination of conventional clear-cutting, the maintenance of biological diversity, and the inclusion of local and First Nations input in management decisions. Some environmental groups endorsed the report, but the Friends of Clayoquot Sound refused, maintaining that there should be no logging of any old-growth forest in Clayoquot. A study by the environmental group Ecotrust found that very little further logging would be possible if panel recommendations were fully implemented, which they have not been to date.

In 1997 the forest giant MacMillan Bloedel turned over the Clayoquot segment of its Tree Farm Licence 44 to a new company, 51 percent of which is controlled by Central Region Nuu-chah-nulth First Nations. The company was called Iisaak, the Nuu-chah-nulth word for "respect." Iisaak struggles to run a profitable business while still honouring commitments to stop clear-cutting, to stay away from pristine watersheds and to foster development of higher-value forest products, among other things. Although their approach has earned the cautious approval of some environmental groups, others point out that Iisaak is still not meeting all of its commitments. Still, there is no doubt that it has significantly improved the type of logging done in Clayoquot Sound.

Many people thought that Clayoquot Sound was finally saved in May 2000 when it was officially designated a World Biosphere Reserve by the United Nations Educational, Scientific and Cultural Organization (UNESCO). Unfortunately, this is not quite the case. A Biosphere Reserve is not a park and is not directly protected, although such a designation no doubt enhances protection efforts. Clayoquot is Canada's 12th region to receive UNESCO Biosphere status, and the first one for British Columbia. The Clayoquot Biosphere Reserve includes both marine and

land areas, extending from Esowista Peninsula in the south to Estevan Point on the southwestern tip of the Hesquiat Peninsula, an area of nearly 350,000 hectares. A Biosphere designation is intended to help strike a balance between conservation and sustainable development, so that communities may survive and industry may flourish while promoting values of wilderness conservation. An important intention of the UNESCO Biosphere Reserve designation is that opportunities for research, education and training be provided within the reserve, and the federal government has put up $12 million toward this work.

Many conservationists remain fixated on the large, intact forests that remain under the threat of logging in Clayoquot. That is a serious concern, but it shouldn't obscure the fact that much good has transpired here. At the time of the major protests of 1993, over 21 percent of Clayoquot's productive old-growth forest had already been cut. A decade later this figure had hardly increased, and the protestors can take full credit for that. It is a remarkable testament to a small group with great vision, backed by an army of supporters around the globe. In addition, the conservation movement has generated many beneficial spinoffs. The forest practices prescribed by the Scientific Panel could become a model for environmentally sound logging the world over—if they ever get fully implemented. The growing involvement of First Nations in decision-making and heavy-duty economic activities must be welcomed by all. The Clayoquot debate raised environmental consciousness and served as an example to conservationists elsewhere in Canada and abroad.

Achieving balance in the Clayoquot biosphere will require sensitivity as light as a feather.

And now, the Biosphere Reserve project offers the hope of bringing all the Clayoquot stakeholders together in an atmosphere of cooperation that just might result in that elusive state of balance, that equilibrium that has been missing since the day in 1774 when the Hesquiaht espied the billowing sails of the *Santiago*.

Will this wished-for equilibrium materialize? If it does, will it be enough to guarantee a full and fruitful life for our little cedar seedling? One may only hope.

9
Recreation on the Edge

Vancouver Island's wild western edge offers recreational opportunities for those who want just a taste of the wilderness, as well as those who want to immerse themselves in it.

Undisturbed nature is Clayoquot's ultimate attraction. Here a solo kayaker paddles near Megin River mouth.

Among the countless options for a day outdoors is a stroll on one of the broad beaches, a hike along the many short trails both within and outside the parks, or a paddle in a kayak or dugout canoe. For small-town evening entertainment, there are often films, slide shows, live music and presentations by visiting scientists. Check the notice boards at the post offices and Co-op grocery stores in Tofino and Ucluelet to see what is happening.

For more of a taste of the wildness, Clayoquot Sound, Barkley Sound and Strathcona Park provide many options for extended wilderness trips, either sea kayaking or hiking. Many guiding companies and tourism operators are based in Tofino and Ucluelet. I strongly recommend that you travel with a guide, even if you are experienced in wilderness travel. The guide is not there simply to help you read a map and keep from getting lost. Guides enrich your experience by providing you with lots of local information and nature interpretation, while at the same time ensuring that your impact on this environment and its wildlife is minimized. Contact the local Visitors' Centres for more information about tourism operators who offer services suited to your needs.

GETTING HERE

Tofino and Ucluelet are on the west coast of Vancouver Island, and can be reached by road or by air. Travel by ferry to either Nanaimo or Victoria. From Nanaimo head north, and turn west on Highway 4, through Port Alberni. No services are available for about 100 kilometres after Port Alberni, so make sure you have fuelled up. Much of the route is narrow and winding, so count on a driving time of between three and four hours to reach either Tofino or Ucluelet from Nanaimo. Please use the pullouts to allow faster vehicles to pass.

Several bus companies and small commuter airlines serve Tofino and Ucluelet from Vancouver, Victoria and Seattle. Contact the Visitors' Centres for current services.

ACCOMMODATION

Places to stay in Tofino and Ucluelet range from basic campgrounds and RV sites, to hostels and motels, to beachside B&Bs and vacation homes, to world-class luxury resorts. During the summer months, everything is booked well ahead of time, so make sure you have your accommodation reserved before you drive all the way out here. Contact the Visitors' Centres by telephone or Internet to find out what options suit you.

SHORT HIKES AND DAY TRIPS

There are many short hikes in the area. "A Guide to Pacific Rim Trails," a small booklet that describes all of these trails in detail and provides useful access maps, is available from the Raincoast Interpretive Centre and other retail outlets in Tofino and Ucluelet.

Top: With red-rimmed eyes and jackhammer bills, restless black oyster-catchers are the clowns of the seashore.

Above: Two-time Canadian women's champion, local surfer Jenny Stewart runs Surf Sister, a Tofino-based surfing school.

There is something about a sandy beach that stirs the youthful imagination.

Previous page: Since 1999, park rangers have reported sharp increases in wolf sightings and wolf-human encounters.

Long Beach

The string of wide, wave-washed beaches at **Long Beach**, all within **Pacific Rim National Park Reserve**, is the star attraction of the West Coast. The uninterrupted stretch of more than 10 kilometres of sand from Schooner Cove, through Long Beach and Combers Beach to Wickaninnish Beach, calls for anyone wanting to do a long beach walk, or a run or bike ride. If you have a good knowledge of the tides and an awareness of ocean swell, on some days it is possible to make your way over the headlands and continue northwest of Schooner Cove.

There are also numerous short interpretive walking trails within Pacific Rim National Park. **The Schooner Trail** is a one-kilometre boardwalk path leading to the beach through both second-growth and old-growth forest. **The Rainforest Trail** consists of two one-kilometre boardwalk loops, with interpretive signs about the rainforest ecosystem. **The Shore Pine Bog** is an 800-metre boardwalk loop through coastal bog. From the **Wickaninnish Interpretive Centre** there are two trails. A short 800-metre trail follows the shoreline to **South Beach**, which has spectacular wave action, especially during winter storms. The 2.5-kilometre **Wickaninnish Trail** passes mostly through rain forest to Florencia Bay. These and other park trails are all described in "A Guide to Pacific Rim Trails."

Wolves in Pacific Rim National Park Reserve

Wolves have inhabited the area that is now Pacific Rim National Park Reserve for millennia. However, since 1999, park rangers have recorded sharp increases in wolf sightings and wolf–human interactions. The wolves are wild, but as they get more used to people they become bolder and may get aggressive. As with bears, if people feed wolves, they become habituated to humans and actually seek them out. This often results in an aggressive encounter, and ultimately to destruction of the wolf.

Wolves inhabit most of the outer coast of Vancouver Island. More wolf–human interactions occur in the park, mainly because more humans frequent this area. Dogs tend to attract wolves, and even large dogs have been killed by wolves in the park.

What you can do to avoid problems with wolves:
- Do not feed wolves, or any other wildlife.
- Keep campsites and picnic areas clean, and put food away promptly.
- Keep your dog on a leash (it is a park regulation anyway).

Please respect all of our wildlife and their habitat.

Ucluelet Area

Kennedy Lake is a good destination for those wanting to swim at a fresh-water beach. Access is along rough gravel roads; refer to the trail guide booklet or a map that shows logging roads for access points. **The Norm Godfrey Nature Trail** is located near the outlet of the lake into Kennedy River. This one-kilometre boardwalk loop showcases some ancient old-growth cedar trees, and provides access to a small, sandy swimming beach. A camping area with an outhouse is located a few kilometres away, down the West Main logging road.

Another short, easy rainforest trail is **"A Walk in the Forest."** The one-kilometre interpretive trail provides information on rainforest ecology as well as on local logging and reforestation methods. The trailhead is signposted, one kilometre toward Port Alberni from the Tofino–Ucluelet junction.

In **Ucluelet**, several new trails have been developed recently on the Ucluth

Peninsula's outer shore; eventually these trails will be connected all the way out to Florencia Bay. The **Wild Pacific Trail** is a 2.7-kilometre loop with breathtaking views of the island-studded entrance to Barkley Sound, and of the wave-bashed rocks far below. The trail passes by Amphitrite Lighthouse, and is definitely a good storm-watching location. The trail ends at He-Tin-Kis Park, and from here you can either follow the He-Tin-Kis trail back to the road, from which it is only a few minutes' walk back to where you started, or you can retrace your steps along the coast. **Another Ucluelet trail** leads from the end of Bay Street to Big Beach. The easy 600-metre trail leads to a beach edged by rocky tide pools. The area is known for its hazardous waves, so be cautious around the rocks and don't turn your back to the waves.

Above: A bright red sea star lies stranded on the beach at low tide.

Left: Clayoquot Sound holds endless adventure for sea kayakers.

Tofino Area

In Tofino, the **Tofino Village Trail** leads to beautiful Tonquin Beach, which looks out toward Wickaninnish Island and Echachist. The short, boardwalk trail leaves from Tonquin Park Road (about a 10-minute walk up 1st Street from downtown Tofino), winds up through rain forest, then drops down to the beach. This is a nice spot from which to watch the sunset in winter. (In summer the sun sets too far to the north—watch it from the Tofino docks.) While in Tofino, also check in with the **Raincoast Interpretive Centre** for current events. They frequently offer interpretive walks guided by local naturalists.

From Tofino you can also get to the **Big Tree Trail** on nearby **Meares Island**. Numerous water taxis are available to drop you off on the island, and local kayak and canoe companies also lead trips to the trail. A 400-metre boardwalk takes you past some of the largest western red cedars in Canada. From the end of the boardwalk, the more adventurous hiker can continue on a 5-kilometre loop through the rain forest. The trail is muddy and at times hard to find, so allow yourself lots of time to navigate this loop.

On the Water

No trip to the West Coast is complete without getting on or in the water.

From both Tofino and Ucluelet, numerous companies offer sea-kayaking trips, whale-watching trips in both open and covered boats, and fishing charters. **Whale-watching** goes on between March and October, but the ocean is calmest in the summer. Call the local Visitors' Centres for more information. Overnight kayak tours are described in more detail in the section on wilderness trips, below.

In Barkley Sound you can travel back in time on the **MV *Lady Rose*** (723-8313, *www.ladyrosemarine.com*). She sets sail several times a week, passing through Port Alberni, Ucluelet and Bamfield, as well as stopping in several smaller coastal communities.

Not many people will ever have the opportunity to travel in a genuine Native dugout canoe. **Tlaook Cultural Adventures** (725-2656, *www.tlaook.com*), based in Tofino, offers tours in traditional Nuu-chah-nulth canoes. These huge canoes, identical to those used for transporting families for millennia, are comfortable and stable, and a great way to experience the ocean: Tla-o-qui-aht guides tell you about their culture as you go.

Several sport fishing outfitters can get you out on the ocean to fish for salmon, halibut or ling cod. Check in with the local Visitors' Centres for more information about the operators.

For a real getaway, I recommend the **Vargas Island Inn** (725-3309), a short boat ride from Tofino. What it lacks in amenities it more than makes up for in West Coast character. From here you can enjoy a beach campfire with a sunset view of Lone Cone, or hike across the island to beautiful Ahous Bay, where gray whales often feed.

Driftwood piled high on Flores Island beaches bears witness to winter storms.

Tofino Sea-Kayaking Company also offers overnight kayak trips to the inn.

For the bizarre experience of combining wilderness with extreme decadence, there is the **Clayoquot Wilderness Resort**, a floating lodge with luxury tents, in northern Clayoquot Sound (725-2699, *www.wildretreat.com*).

And for getting *in* the water, numerous surf schools in Tofino and Ucluelet offer lessons for beginners, as well as board and wetsuit rentals.

Hot Springs Cove

The natural thermal waters at the ocean's edge in **Hot Springs Cove** are part of **Maquinna Provincial Marine Park**. They can be reached by boat from Tofino (one to one and a half hours each way) or by a 20-minute float plane ride from Tofino. A nice travel combination is to travel one-way on a whale-watching boat or on the Hesquiaht Band's *Matlahaw* Water Taxi (670-1110 or 1-888-781-9977) and one-way by float plane. Day trips to the springs are offered by many of the whale-watching companies based in Tofino. All transport takes you to the Government Dock; from here it is a 20-minute walk along a boardwalk trail through old-growth rain forest to the springs.

Staying overnight near the springs gives you the luxury of enjoying a soak in the evening, after the crowds have left. **The Innchanter** is an 26-metre wooden freighter built in 1927 and refitted as a cozy lodge, anchored near the Government Dock (670-1149, *www.innchanter.com*). **The Hot Springs Lodge** is located in the Hesquiaht village of Hot Springs Cove, a short boat ride from the Government Dock. There is also a campground near the dock, with tent sites and toilets. For information about the lodge or the campground, call 670-1106 or 1-888-781-9977.

Tofino Sea Kayaking Company offers one-week paddling trips from Tofino through Clayoquot Sound, to Hot Springs Cove.

Tlaook Cultural Adventures, based in Tofino, is a native-run business that offers tours in traditional Nuu-chah-nulth dugouts.

Float planes are readily available to carry sightseers to the most inaccessible parts of Clayoquot Sound. Here a plane arrives at Megin Lake.

LONGER WILDERNESS EXCURSIONS

To experience the full magic of wild West Coast nature, you have to put civilization behind you and venture out into the real wilderness, but such excursions are not for everyone and should not be undertaken lightly. The whole region is inhabited by bears, wolves and cougars. All of the animals here swim, and they can show up on even the smallest of islands. Please travel sensibly and responsibly. Do not feed wildlife. Do not leave food in packs or kayaks; hang it in proper bear caches at least 2.5 metres off the ground. Cook below the high-tide line so that food smells are washed away. And be aware of the high-tide mark when choosing your tent site! Please pack out everything you packed in, including toilet paper. For elimination of human waste, it is better to use the intertidal zone: crabs and other critters will decompose your waste much more quickly than if you go in the woods or higher up on the beach.

Kayaking

Several local companies provide overnight tours with qualified sea-kayaking guides. For tours of the **Broken Group**, contact Majestic Ocean Kayaking (726-2868, *www.oceankayaking.com*). For guided tours of **Clayoquot Sound**, contact Tofino Sea-Kayaking Company (725-4222 or 1-800-863-4664, *www.tofino-kayaking.com*). For overnight instructional tours, contact Rainforest Kayak Adventures (725-3117, *www.rainforestkayak.com*).

Kayak rentals are available to experienced paddlers. Although on some days the water may appear calm, it is still the ocean, and wind and waves may appear very rapidly. If you are not experienced in surf skills and rough-water rescues, please paddle with a guide. From **Tofino**, Tofino Sea-Kayaking Company (725-4222 or 1-800-863-4664, *www.tofino-kayaking.com*) offers kayak rentals. No rental kayaks are available in Ucluelet. To rent kayaks to paddle the Broken Group, contact the *Lady Rose* (723-8313, *www.ladyrosemarine.com*).

Hiking

There are hiking trails on Vargas and Flores islands, and in Strathcona Park.

On **Vargas Island**, a five-kilometre trail crosses the island, passing through old-growth rain forest and coastal bog, to the expansive curved beach at Ahous Bay. Wilderness camping (no toilet or other facilities) is permitted at Ahous. You can arrange transport to Vargas Island by any one of Tofino's many water taxis. Access to the trailhead is through private property; you must contact the Vargas Island Inn to arrange permission to pass through (725-3309).

The **Wild Side Heritage Trail** was created and is maintained by the Ahousaht First Nation on **Flores Island**. The trail leaves from **Ahousat** village, and follows about 10 kilometres of shoreline, mostly through wild surf-washed beaches and over rocky headlands, to Cow Bay. From Cow Bay, a rougher trail climbs through the rain forest to the peak of Mount Flores. Wilderness camping (no toilet or other facilities) is permitted along the beaches. You must check in Ahousat for trail information before

Icy meltwater descends from a rock face, forming the headwaters of the Bedwell River.

heading out. Call the Wild Side office (670-9586) or the Ahousaht Band Office about bookings and fees, and to arrange water taxi transport to Ahousat. There is accommodation in Ahousat at the **Hummingbird Hostel** (670-9679) and at **Vera Little's B&B** (670-9511). Ahousaht elder Stanley Sam's *Ahousaht Wild Side Heritage Trail Guidebook* (Western Canada Wilderness Committee, 1997) is a useful resource, with trail maps and lots of cultural information about the traditional owners of the land.

Numerous well-maintained trails are located in **Strathcona Provincial Park**. The park, in the centre of Vancouver Island, is the site of headwaters of rivers that flow northward into Nootka Sound and eastward across the island, as well as southward into Clayoquot Sound. Only the southernmost part of the park officially belongs to Clayoquot; the waters of Baby Bedwell Lake, Bedwell Lake and Little Jim Lake flow into the northern reaches of Clayoquot Sound. It is possible to hike from sea level, up the Bedwell River and into the high country. I do not recommend this route, as the river was logged out decades ago; the long route passes mostly through dense second-growth forest of spindly alder trees. The Moyeha and Megin rivers also lead up from sea level into Strathcona, but there are no trails in these valleys. By road it is about a three-hour drive from Nanaimo to the heart of Strathcona Park; follow Highway 28 west from Campbell River. For more information on hiking in Strathcona, contact BC Parks or visit *http://wlapwww.gov.bc.ca/bcparks/explore/parkpgs/strathco.*

Air Tours

Float planes give scenic tours of Clayoquot and Barkley sounds and fly over the snow-capped peaks of Strathcona Park, as well as offering whale-watching tours. They are also available to charter for dropoffs for fishing trips or one-way kayak trips. In Tofino, contact Atleo Air (725-2205) or Tofino Air (725-4454). In Ucluelet, contact West Coast Wild Adventures (726-7715).

A humpback whale sounds.

CONTACTS

(Area Code is 250 unless otherwise specified):
Tofino Visitor Centre 725-3414
www.tofinobc.org
Ucluelet Visitor Centre 726-4641
www.uclueletinfo.com
Pacific Rim Visitor Centre 726-4600
www.pacificrimvisitor.ca
Raincoast Interpretive Centre 725-2560
www.tofinores.com
Clayoquot Biosphere Trust 726-4715
www.clayoquotbiosphere.org
Friends of Clayoquot Sound 725-4218
www.focs.ca
Pacific Rim National Park Reserve 726-7721
www.pc.gc.ca/pn-np/bc/pacificrim/
National Park Info Line 1-888-773-8888
Camping Reservations 1-877-737-3783

Acknowledgements

So many people have contributed to the creation and completion of *The Wild Edge*. Neil and Marilyn Buckle, Bernard Charleson, Arline Craig, Pipot Dupuis, Lorraine Ennis, Maureen Fraser, Ken Gibson, Walter Guppy, Murray John Sr., Jim Levis, Levi and Carl and especially Joe Martin, Islay MacLeod, Charles and Howard McDiarmid, Tracy Morben, Henry Nolla, Ben Ronnenbergh and Nick Kowall, Rosie Swan and Dave Taron generously provided me with interviews and information. Many others kindly agreed to appear in photographs for the book. John Clague, Jim Darling, Adrian Dorst, Rick Harbo, Bob Hansen, Alan MacMillan, Maryjka Mychajlowycz, Rod Palm, Tom Reimchen and Doug Palfrey have helped with research and fact-checking. Barb Beasley, Neil and Marilyn Buckle, Mark Hobson, Kevin Jordan, Carl Martin, Adrienne Mason, Ralph Tieleman, Linda White and Barb Campbell at the Tofino Library, and Dorothy Baert from Tofino Sea-Kayaking Company have all helped by providing reference materials. Carl Martin, Jackie Prescott and Kathleen Shaw reviewed early drafts of the text. Caron Olive provided the digital maps that serve as the base for the maps in this book. Ronan Lannuzel took the author photo, one I actually like. The editorial and production team at Harbour Publishing—Howard White, Vici Johnstone, Peter Read, Roger Handling, Mary Schendlinger and so many others have made essential contributions to this book. A grant from the Clayoquot Biosphere Trust helped to support me during the writing. Jason Feaver, John Forde and Mark Hobson have provided photos where my own coverage lacked.

In a special category are friends and supporters who have provided inspiration and moral support through the years that went into this book. This project would never even have started without the help of my great friends Douglas Forster and Silvia Heinrich and my Aunt Phyl and Uncle Win Elliott, who have welcomed me into their homes and supported me in many other ways. My Nuu-chah-nulth friends: the Tla-o-qui-aht Martin family and Matthew Williams; the Ahousaht Swan and John and Sam families; and from Hesquiat the Charleson and Ignace families and Mark Mickey and Mabel Sport, have all taught me lots and shared so much. Peter Buckland, John Forde and the Whale Centre, Dag Goering and Maria Coffey, Linda Fuerniss and Pipo Damiano, Margaret Horsfield, Michael Mullin and Dorothy Baert, Kathleen and Gary Shaw, Shaun Shelongosky, Meg Stewart, Ken Thomson and Liz John from Ocean Outfitters, Don Travers and Kati Martini of Remote Passages, Douglas Wright, as well as my friends in the Clayoquot Writers' Group and the amazing core community of Tofino, have given me crucial friendship and support. Tofino's amazing wilderness photographers Adrian Dorst and Mark Hobson have been mentors as well as great friends. A huge thank you to my dearest friends, who have helped me through so much, and without whose support I would never have got here: Natasha Baert, Darryn Brown, Lyne Desrosiers, Bonny Glambeck, Kevin Jordan, Mike Laanela, Paulette Laurendeau, Dan Lewis, Corinne Murray, Fiona Peters, Katrina Peters, Jackie Prescott, Joanna Streetly, George Yearsley, my sister Joanne Windh and all my dear faraway friends overseas. And an extra thank you to Valerie Langer for being the type of person who, when she sees something that she can help with or fix, just does it; and to my Bedstemor, whose gift to me nearly 20 years ago bought me the camera equipment that I still use today. Finally, thanks to my Mom for encouraging my interest in nature, and to my Dad for encouraging my interest in photography. Every one of you has made a difference. Thank you, all.

To the defenders of Clayoquot and other wild lands and waters.
Your vision and your sacrifices give us all a future.

In memoriam: Henry Nolla, 1930–2004, who has been so much to so many.

Index

Published by
Harbour Publishing Co. Ltd.
P.O. Box 219
Madeira Park, BC
V0N 2H0
www.harbourpublishing.com

Cover and text design by Roger Handling
Printed and bound in Canada

Harbour Publishing acknowledges financial support from the Government of Canada through the Book Publishing Industry Development Program and the Canada Council for the Arts, and from the Province of British Columbia through the British Columbia Arts Council and the Book Publisher's Tax Credit through the Ministry of Provincial Revenue.

Library and Archives Canada Cataloguing in Publication

Windh, Jacqueline, 1964-
 The wild edge : Clayoquot, Long Beach & Barkley Sound / Jacqueline Windh.

Includes index.
ISBN 1-55017-350-2

 1. Clayoquot Sound Region (B.C.)—Pictorial works. 2. Long Beach (B.C.)—Pictorial works. 3. Barkley Sound Region (B.C.)—Pictorial works. I. Title.

FC3844.4.W56 2004   917.11'2044'0222   C2004-903103-1

VARGAS I.

MEARES I.

FORTUNE CHANNEL

KAKAWIS

KELTSEMAT

OPITSAT

TOFINO INLET

STUBBS I. **TOFINO**

BROWNING PASSAGE

WICKANINNISH I.

MacKenzie
Beach

INDIAN I.

ECHACHIS I.

Middle
Beach

GRICE BAY

Chesterman
Beach

LENNARD I.

FRANK I.

Cox Bay

ESOWISTA

Long
Beach

SCHOONER COVE

Combers
Beach

WICKANINNISH   BAY

Wickaninnish
Beach

FLORENCIA B

0 km   Scale in kilometres   10 km